Jeni Archileck.

Flower Arranging

COLLINS NUTSHELL BOOKS

Flower Arranging

JANE DERBYSHIRE

With Photographs and Line Drawings

COLLINS
LONDON AND GLASGOW

GENERAL EDITOR: J. B. FOREMAN, M.A.
First published 1964
Latest Reprint 1968

For

HELEN JANE and SUSAN

PRINTED IN GREAT BRITAIN
BY COLLINS CLEAR-TYPE PRESS

Contents

CHAPTER 1

What is Flower Arranging?

In the modern world, with its varied interests, hurry and noise, its almost non-stop radio and TV, and its thousands of working women, it is perhaps surprising that the hobby of arranging flowers is more popular than ever before. Women have always brought flowers indoors to brighten their homes, taken them to cheer up invalids, and used them to decorate churches, but in the past the flowers were picked or bought rather haphazardly and popped quickly into vases which were often quite unsuitable.

Our eyes are now open to the fascinating variety of foliage and blooms and the endless ways of mixing them. This book is mostly about flowers to decorate and beautify the home, but I have also dealt with the enjoyment of flower clubs and the excitement of exhibiting, as so many women are taking up the competitive side of the hobby. More than 70,000 people are members of clubs and societies affiliated to the National Association of Flower Arrangement Societies of Great Britain.

Nowhere in this book do I intend to sound dogmatic; we are all individuals, and so are all flowers. A dozen daffodils arranged by one person will never look exactly the same as when arranged by someone else, just as no two women produce exactly the same cake from a given recipe. Yet certain principles have been evolved which, if followed, lead to pleasing and successful flower arrangements. If you are a beginner, information about these basic principles is what you need most. I hope this book will be of special value to those taking up the hobby, for I have tried to remember my own novice days. The more experienced will find, I trust, some new ideas.

But first, let's look at the elements of modern flower arranging.

Ten Golden Rules

1. Nowadays full use is made of the almost limitless variety of natural plant material. There has been an expansion of thought on what is suitable to include in "flower" designs. It is now quite usual to see vegetables and fruits included with flowers, as well as things like shapely seedheads, driftwood, and preserved leaves.

2. Care is taken in the treatment and preparation of flowers and other materials before they are arranged. In this way they are given the longest possible life. Flowers and leaves once considered useless when cut, because of their tendency to flag quickly, can now be included in arrangements.

3. Flower containers are different nowadays. No longer are we limited to vases and bowls. The term "container" is taken to mean anything at all which will hold water and in which flowers may be arranged. This new conception has opened the way to countless new and exciting flower arrangements. Everyday things around the home—from the kitchen cupboard as well as from the china cabinet—are acceptable as containers.

4. The style of the room in which the arrangement is to stand is taken into account, for there are many basic kinds of arrangements from which to choose. Formal arrangements harmonise with antique furniture and period-style homes. Simple mass arrangements go with cottage rooms. Sophisticated "line" designs fit in happily with ultra-modern furnishings and decor. Between these

extremes, flower arrangements can be made to blend with, and enhance, any mode of architecture, furniture and decoration.

5. The creation of planned designs means that flowers and leaves must stay in their appointed positions. This is made possible by the use of wire netting, gadgets called pinholders, and water-retaining material such as Oasis, all of which enable the stems to be arranged in any desired position.

6. Colour is an important element in a flower arrangement. Not only are the hues and shades of blooms and leaves blended or contrasted harmoniously but they are also chosen to complement the container and the setting in which the arrangement is to be seen.

7. Stems of flowers and leaves are not used necessarily at their natural length. They are almost always cut down to fit the design.

8. Flower arrangements are designed for the particular position in which they are to stand. This emphasis on *design* is perhaps the most striking and important difference between the old and modern ways of doing the flowers. A modern arrangement has a definite shape or silhouette.

9. As well as the shape when seen from the front, with its attractive proportions of width and height, a modern flower arrangement also has *depth*. Some flowers are brought forward, others placed farther back, to give a 3-D effect.

10. Every flower, leaf, or twig used in a modern arrangement is put in to play its part in the design, instead of at random. One effect of this is that pleasing arrangements can be made with very little material. Used to their best advantage, three flowers can be as effective as three dozen.

Flowers at Home

Although flowers are arranged everywhere and for all sorts of occasions, their special place is in home decoration. To look their best, flower arrangements must blend with the room, or with the piece of furniture on which they are placed.

Some rooms are badly proportioned, and flowers can improve them. A wall which seems too high can, for example, be made to appear shorter and wider if a low flower arrangement is placed against it. On the other hand, a tall, slim spire of flowers can make a room seem higher when the ceiling is low. Designing flower arrangements helps to cultivate an eye not only for good proportion but also for colour blending and general good taste in decorations.

There are three traditional spots for cut flowers in the average home: 1. A vase in a window; 2. On the dining-table; 3. In a jug on the hall table or window ledge. Yet there *are* other and better places. Consider the dozen and one natural focal points about a home where the eye rests for a moment; take advantage of these by positioning an arrangement at one of these points.

The fireplace, for instance. The hearth is the centre of family life, and in the summer it will take a large, dramatic flower design. (Guard against the flowers' dislike of draughts by blocking up the chimney mouth with hardboard.)

Study Your Home

Why not study your home and its layout? If there is a half landing at the turn of the stairs, large enough to take a chest or table, this is a point where flowers will be happily conspicuous—and they'll last well, too. The mantelpiece is a good position on autumn and winter days, when colourfully preserved leaves, flowers, cones, evergreens and berries will survive quite happily. The television top is another excellent place, while a table right opposite a door is far better than one which is hidden every time the door is opened.

A coffee table may be the centrepiece when friends call; a small, pretty arrangement here will always draw admiration. Similarly, a simple posy on a guest's bedside table or an invalid's breakfast tray will not go unobserved. When friends drop in for drinks, present an unusual decoration, such as red and flame geranium blooms with grapes and a few leaves in a dark green wine bottle on the sideboard or drinks table. Flower designs look lovely when seen against the wood of a sideboard or side table, whether it is old well-polished mahogany or one of the modern light-hued woods. Use flowers throughout the house, not just in the living-room, when they are in plentiful supply, and at other times use dried or preserved materials, as described later in this book.

Flowers in Windows

Though I suppose it will always be popular, a window is not a specially good setting in which to stand cut flowers. Certainly they look pretty from outside, but so do flowering pot plants, which are much better suited to this position. Cut flowers in a window are exposed to the sun during the day and to sudden chills at night, as well as to draughts, and they invariably have a shorter life than flowers placed elsewhere in the room.

When the curtains are drawn at night a flower arrangement in the window will be either shut out or else be seen as a confused design against the curtains if they are patterned. Leave the curtains open, however, and the arrangement will be shown dramatically against the darkness of the panes, which reflect like a mirror. Pink, white, or clear yellow flowers look wonderful with the night as a backcloth.

A well-defined shape is always important when an arrangement is to stand in a window. This is because it is seen mainly in silhouette from inside the house.

Where To Do the Flowers

Where is the best place to actually make a flower arrangement? Certainly the best way is to do the arrangement on the spot, where it is to stand, because it is much easier to get the size, shape, and colours right for the setting.

In the end, of course, experience will be your best guide. If you find you are happiest when sitting at the kitchen table with a cup of coffee handy, and plenty of room to spread out the flowers, then this will be where your best work will be achieved. But do first take your chosen container to the place where the arrangement is to be seen, and check that the container is the right size, shape and colour. Then roughly put in the outline shape of flowers and leaves before going elsewhere to complete the design. In this way your arrangement will be in pleasing proportion to the room and the exact position it is to occupy.

Wherever you choose to work you will need some kind of protection for carpets and tables. Have your flowers in a bucket of water at your feet, and spread out sheets of newspaper round about on which to drop the cut-off stems, rejected flowers, bits of twig and other waste. When you've finished, the rubbish can be carried straight out to the dustbin. An even better protection for the floor is a large old piece of thick curtaining. A sheet of plastic material is useful to protect the table top.

Polished surfaces may be damaged by water syphoned out of a flower container by leaves and flower stems. So be warned—always put some sort of protective material under the container when the arrangement is completed. You can use a piece of leather cloth, or better still water-resisting plastic material with a wood grain finish. The material should be cut a few inches larger than the base of the container. It's a good idea to keep a selection of different sizes.

Relaxing with Flowers

Does it all sound rather frightening so far? Believe me, it isn't really. There can be few more enjoyable ways of relaxing than with flowers, enjoying their shapes, textures and colours, and their scents. Don't worry at all if, in the early days, the shape goes completely wrong and the colours seem to fight each other.

Follow the rules, keep trying, and every new arrangement will be a little better than the last. There is no "Open Sesame," but once you have mastered the guiding principles your skill will very rapidly grow. You'll find flower arranging becoming a source of greater and greater pleasure and satisfaction.

CHAPTER 2

How It All Began

To gain an understanding of flower arranging it is interesting to take a backward glance to the beginnings of the art. In the Orient, formal flower arranging goes back hundreds of years, and the skill has long been a part of home decoration in Japan. This extreme form of the art demands some years of study by its devotees, and is usually something of an acquired taste to Western people. Many women in Britain do study the Japanese technique, but the majority prefer a more English style.

A Long Tradition

We in Britain have a traditional love of cut flowers and foliage. It is closely linked with worship, gardening, house decoration and personal adornment. The ancient Druids picked mistletoe for their religious rites, and when the Romans came to Britain they introduced flower festivals such as those dedicated to Flora, the Goddess of Spring.

For centuries after the Romans, it was customary for people to go into the countryside at the beginning of May and bring home branches and flowers, which they made into garlands. These were hung outside the house, near the door, as good luck tokens.

In parts of rural Derbyshire to this day ceremonies of dressing the wells with cut flowers still take place. On the appointed day the village wells are exquisitely decorated, each with a life-size religious picture and text composed of countless thousands of flowers, mosses, seedheads, cones and a variety of other natural plant life. Often, just the petals of flowers are used. These are set in damp clay, which keeps them fresh for about a week. Well-dressing most probably had its ancient beginnings in the worship of water spirits.

Flowers In Church

The custom of decorating churches on Sundays and saints' days also has ancient roots. Special flowers were designated to particular saints, and on each saint's day altars were strewn with the appropriate blooms. In the Middle Ages, flowers with a medicinal use were consecrated to favourite saints; there are still books in existence which list them.

To-day's flower arrangers could quite properly include an arrangement of a saint's own flower when doing the flowers in church. For example, London Pride is one of St. Patrick's flowers; it was once known as St. Patrick's Cabbage.

Although the early church decorations were merely flowers strewn, or else hung in swags, it must soon have occurred to people that water would make them last longer, and so flowers and foliage came to be arranged in a simple way.

Early Instances of Flowers Indoors

Flowers began to be brought into the home. Sweet-smelling blooms and herbs were cut and brought indoors, along with reeds and straw, to be strewn on the earthen floors. The flowers and herbs helped to mask the odour of decaying refuse, in those days flung out into the streets. Obviously the best place for flowers to help sweeten the air was in the window or near the door, so women began

15

to place them there, in water so that they would last for a day or two. It was firmly believed that flowers' scents gave protection from disease, and posies were worn and carried for this reason, especially by the well-to-do. High Court judges carried nosegays as a protection against gaol fever.

Down the centuries fresh flowers were worn by men in their buttonholes and by women to trim their hair, hats and gowns; thrifty wives would realise that these flowers could be used again if kept in water. Yearly rents for land and houses were sometimes paid wholly or partly in cut flowers; roses are specifically mentioned in many old records. One such lease dates back to 1352, and there are instances of this strange form of token rent being paid to the present day. It isn't too hard to imagine the wives of the flower-loving landlords arranging the rental roses. So, in churches and homes, people began to arrange flowers.

Vases Were Unknown

At first, vases were unknown. Flowers were placed in jugs, glasses, and bottles, as can be seen from old paintings. The vase, as a specially designed container for flowers, seems not to have come into use until about 1400. Later on, flower containers were readily available, and some were imported from the Continent. People began to grow flowers and herbs especially for picking, and street sellers began to hawk them.

Three hundred years ago Izaak Walton wrote of "an honest ale house" where he proposed to entertain a friend. "We shall find a cleanly room with lavender in the window," he told him. Country women and children found it worthwhile to pick wild flowers as well as garden blooms, which they carried in baskets to nearby towns and sold in the markets to people who used them to decorate their homes.

As late as Edwardian times little girls were often to be heard demanding "A pin to see a peepshow," the peepshow being a miniature arrangement of roses or geraniums and grasses pressed between two squares of glass. The delicately arranged flower "pictures" were contained in envelopes, each envelope having its front cut open to form a window. Neat skill in fashioning cowslip and primrose balls and daisy chains is still passed on in some country districts.

The Language of Flowers

One hopes that the ancient custom of men giving cut flowers to their wives and girl friends will continue for ever. I have a Georgian children's book which shows countrymen presenting posies to their best girls. Flower-giving reached a high fever in Victorian times, when every flower had its special meaning and it was possible to send quite complicated romantic messages by means of a carefully selected bunch of mixed flowers.

From old paintings and books it is clear that flowers, particularly garden ones, were used in water to decorate the homes of rich and poor alike from early times. But it was after the Industrial Revolution, and in our Victorian grandmothers' youth, that flowers really entered the home in a grand way. Smaller houses and cottages kept to the traditional ways with cut flowers, placing them simply in Staffordshire figures and cheap vases and jugs. Elsewhere the story was changing.

Women of the upper and middle classes had little to occupy them; they had ample staffs to cope with all the work of their homes. They had time on their hands and they entertained. The flowers throughout the house were generally arranged daily (the water in each vase had to be changed every day, it was believed) by the lady of the house or one of her daughters.

New Species from Abroad

Wealthy townsfolk moved to the outskirts, where land was plentiful and available to be made into large gardens. The gardeners produced a wealth of blooms for the women of the household to arrange, and cut flowers were used in large quantities as never before. At the same time, many new species and varieties were being introduced to Britain from abroad, and the homes of the wealthy boasted conservatories and glasshouses filled with exotic flowers and attractive foliage plants. The most elaborate designs of flower and leaf were attempted by head gardeners for luncheon and dinner parties. Good society generally regarded hot-house blooms as "the thing," especially when decorating formal dinner tables.

There were vogues for shallow pool effects, using either real water or pieces of mirror glass. Three-tier glass tazzas were piled high with fruit and flowers. Real miniature fountains and blocks of ice were introduced at the table, then had their day and passed out of favour. Intricate patterns of flowers and leaves arranged directly on the tablecloth became popular, and there was a fashion for many large and small bowls of flowers and plants grouped in the centre of the table on cloths of satin, silk, coloured damask and brocade.

Flowers and Food

For winter room decoration dried bulrushes, "Chinese lanterns," and pampas grass were much liked, and the small wild grasses were collected and carefully arranged, particularly in rural areas. There was a "natural school"

which advocated the use of simple blossoms and leaves
from the hedgerows and snippets from the vegetable
garden.

A flower and food book was published in the early part
of the 19th century for "women of good taste and judgment"; it gave dozens of ideas for matching flowers to
the food to be served. For instance, an idea for "A Mad
March Hare luncheon" had a centrepiece made with "a
large round box, two inches high, filled with moist sand."
Readers were told: "Arrange in the sand jonquils to give
the effect of waving growing flowers. In the middle of this
put a stuffed hare. The candles should be capped with
matching yellow shades, the whole to be laid on a cloth of
soft green linen. The first course to be chilled grapes
served on nests of spun sugar resting upon natural leaves.
A subsequent course to be of hare." Another recipe for a
successful table layout, from the same book, suggests
masses of pink roses in horse-shoe shape as the table
centrepiece, the meal being chosen to match the flowers—
pink ices, pink wines, rose-red bon-bons and lamb.

Flowers were often used "with great care as to effect"
decoratively upon the food itself as it was brought to the
table. There are recipes for potato salads in daisy shapes,
and cakes made to look like peach blossoms, the appropriate real flowers being used in the arrangements to link
up the theme. Both the table and hostess's gown were
sometimes flower-decorated to match.

To Hold the Stems

Even a hundred years ago there were stirrings of the need
to get the flowers to stand upright in the centre of a vase or
to be held in position lower down and over the rim. In a
collection of old flower books which I have, there are
occasional references to "contrivances on the market

which will enable flowers to be placed more attractively"
and I have some antique china containers with domed
tops which are pierced with holes to take flower stems at
various angles.

Mrs. C. W. Earle, the Victorian writer, published
Pot-pourri from a Surrey Garden in the 1890's. She had
been making a study of things which last well in water and
had successfully arranged bamboo leaves "in a Japanese
pattern" on her dinner table after soaking them all day in
water.

She was interested in the Japanese way with flowers,
and frequently used bamboo wedges inside her vases to
hold the stalks firmly. She urged the use of fewer flowers
in arrangements, than was customary at the time.

A few years later (1907) another author took these ideas
a stage farther. She was Gertrude Jekyll, the famous
gardening writer, one of the first people to discover "the
convenience of galvanised wire netting." In a book on
flower arranging she suggests that wire netting should be
used "like scaffoldings, placed in the vase in two tiers, the
two tiers being kept in shape by stout wire legs soldered
on by any handy village blacksmith."

Wire netting (or chicken wire) is still considered one of
the best means of holding stems in position, particularly
for massed flower designs, yet some women still struggle on
without its aid, buying any gadget but this simple and
cheap one.

New Ideas Introduced

Between the two World Wars a number of writers in this
country produced books on the art of flower arranging.
Notable among them was Constance Spry, whose name is
synonymous with the "free" English style of arranging.

After the last War, when women had picked up their

normal lives again, and gardens which had been vigor-
ously "dug for victory" were replanted with flowers, a
fresh wave of enthusiasm for arranging flowers came in.
New ideas were introduced into Britain from the United
States, South Africa, and other countries, and some of
these were adapted to our particular taste and conditions.
Lecturers and demonstrators appeared, to pass on knowledge to the rapidly-growing flower arranging clubs.

And so to the present day. From great buildings all
decked out for a Royal occasion—with microphones and
TV cameras hidden away in the flower arrangements—
to the bar of the pub in the small-town High Street, women
everywhere are "doing the flowers" with extraordinary
skill and charm. For the first time, the ordinary woman is
attempting and producing flower arrangements which are
works of art in their own right.

We are still on the crest of the wave—who knows what
the future holds?

CHAPTER 3

The Equipment You Need

What do you need to start flower arranging? Well, this is one of the few hobbies you can begin with very little equipment. It can cost almost anything you wish, from a few coppers to many pounds, depending entirely on yourself. A beginner can more often than not begin right away with an expenditure of only a few coppers (for a bit of chicken wire).

Everyone has some sort of container which will do to start with, if it's only a jug or a vegetable dish, and flowers and leaves are usually available from the garden, the countryside, or the shops.

Some medium is required for holding the stems in place and at the desired angles in the container. There are several methods and gadgets; these are sometimes called the mechanics of the arrangement, and they are as follows:

Chicken Wire

First there is chicken wire (wire netting), the cheapest yet most valuable asset to the modern flower arranger. Buy the very least expensive kind; this is because it has to be crumpled up, and the higher the price the stronger and stiffer, and more difficult to handle, it will be. Ask for two-inch gauge. You don't need to buy a whole roll (as I mistakenly thought as a beginner!). About a yard of it, from any ironmonger's, is enough for a start.

Cut off the "selvedge" edge, with pliers or florist's scissors, and throw it away. To use the netting, cut off a section measuring about one-and-a-half times the size of the top of the chosen container. (*See* fig. 1.) There are various ways of placing the netting inside the container. The method I have found most satisfactory is to roll the netting into a loose "Swiss roll" shape.

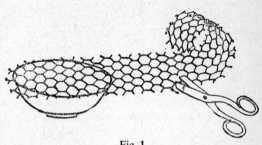

Fig. 1

Press the roll into the container, keeping as many as possible of the cut ends of wire near the top. Some of these cut ends can now be bent over the rim of the container to keep the netting firmly in position. Allow some of the netting to come an inch or so higher than the rim. (*See* fig. 2.)

Chicken wire is indispensable when one is using many flowers and other material together in what is called a "mass" arrangement. The wire will keep even heavy branches in position, but is equally suitable, when more closely crumpled, for miniature arrangements.

No part of the wire must be visible when the design is completed; if it shows, cover it with leaves, flowers, or moss recessed among the principal flowers.

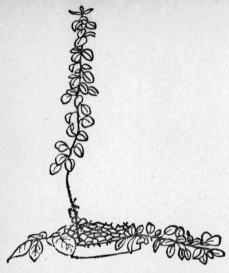

Fig. 2

Choose a Good Pinholder

Pinholders can be bought from most florist's shops these days. They cost anything from 1s. 6d. (for the smallest) upwards. A pinholder is simply a flat piece of metal, usually lead, in which rows of strong pins are embedded to hold the stems of flowers and leaves. Pinholders come in all sorts of shapes and sizes; some have a base in the form of a rubber suction cup, but in my experience these are less satisfactory than the metal kind. Avoid also the

24

Fig. 3

models in which the pins are spaced wide apart. When buying a pinholder, choose one with really sharp-pointed pins of about three-quarters of an inch in length; too short pins will not hold stems reliably. A good metal pinholder should feel heavy in the hand in relation to its size, and it's also a good idea to test for loose and blunt pins before handing over your money.

Like everything else, the best and most expensive pinholders usually work out cheapest in the long run. Don't try to economise on size, for it is vital that your pinholder should be large enough to take comfortably all the stems in the arrangement you are creating. One which is too small for the job in hand will merely frustrate you—and handicap you unnecessarily.

You can choose between round, square, oblong and crescent-shaped pinholders, according to the shape of the container you are using. Now readily available are pinholders complete with a holder for water, just deep enough to allow the water to cover the pins. These come into their own when you need a very small container which is easy to conceal.

Pinholders are generally used in shallow containers (see fig. 3), and for big arrangements in deep containers it is an advantage to use them in conjunction with chicken wire. Although pinholders will last for many years (I have some which are ten years old) the pins sometimes go blunt and out of alignment through constant use, so making them only semi-efficient. It really pays to throw out a pin-holder which is in bad shape, with loose, bent, or blunt pins. After using a pinholder, clean out any bits of broken stem or decayed leaf caught between the pins; you can do this quite easily with a metal skewer or with scissors. Rinse under a tap, and dry thoroughly in front of the fire or over a radiator before putting away.

Modelling Clay

Pinholders are stuck into position in containers with three blobs of modelling clay, Plasticine, or Stemfix Sealing Strip. (See fig. 4). The fixing material is first softened by rubbing it between the hands. It must hold the pinholder limpet-firm to the container, and it will not do this if either the clay, the container, or the pinholder is not ab-solutely dry. Put the blobs of the fixing material on the underside of the pinholder, then cover the pins with a thickly folded cloth to protect your hand and firmly

26

press the pinholder to the container, giving a small screw-turn as you do so.

The reason for sticking the pinholder to the container is to ensure that, as you add flowers and foliage in the arrangement, the top-heavy weight does not pull the pinholder over. Consequently, it is most important to make sure that the pinholder is completely anchored before you start the arrangement.

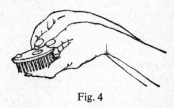

Fig. 4

Even with these precautions a pinholder will sometimes break away from its moorings and the arrangement will begin to fall forwards. Correct this by putting a weight on the pinholder at the back. (*See* fig. 5.) For this purpose you can use a spare pinholder, a heavy pair of scissors, or one of the weights from the kitchen scales. I have even saved the day by looping a length of heavy gauge florist's wire round the pinholder and hooking the other end of the wire back over the rim of the container.

Chicken Wire Plus Pinholder
A little crumpled wire netting, pressed on to the pins of a pinholder, is a good way of adapting it to accommodate more stems than it was designed to carry. This method is

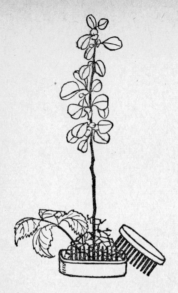

Fig. 5

useful, too, for providing extra support when heavy stems of shrubs, fruit blossoms, and similar material are to be arranged. It works also when including the slim leaves of flowers grown from bulbs (tulips, daffodils, etc.). These leaves are very pliable and are half-hearted about standing up for themselves when impaled on a pinholder. The extra bit of security they gain from the wire netting makes all the difference. (*See* fig. 6.)

Fig. 6

Putty and Lead

Putty makes a splendid base for holding driftwood and similar heavy material in position. It will stay fresh and serviceable for some time if you keep it wrapped in a plastic bag when not in use. A strip of plumber's lead is handy to have around for use as a counterweight, either as an anchor for an insecure pinholder or at the bottom or back of a very light and unstable container.

Stemfix and Oasis

Florist's shops sell several different kinds of water-retaining material, of which two of the best-known are Stemfix and Oasis, specially made for flower arranging. They are more convenient than wire netting or a pinholder in a fragile glass or porcelain container, or in a container which will not hold water.

29

Stemfix is green in colour, and can be used in two ways. In the first method, the whole block as purchased is put into a pail or bowl of water and weighted down. It is left under water and when it is thoroughly saturated, pieces can be cut off in the sizes needed for any container. The top of the Stemfix should be about an inch higher than the rim of the container.

Arrange your flowers straight into the Stemfix; all but the finest and thinnest stems will push into it with ease. Fine stems sometimes need to have holes made for them with a knitting or darning needle. Stemfix will hold stems at any desired angle, and unless conditions are abnormally hot, will retain enough moisture to provide all that is necessary for several days. A piece of chicken wire, cut to fit like a guard over the Stemfix, and hooked over the container's edge, will prevent heavy stalks breaking pieces out of the block. When the flowers die it is simple to remove them from the Stemfix, which can then be re-soaked and used again.

A Second Way

After Stemfix has been used a few times the block will become too broken up for further service. This is when the second method comes into its own (though it can also be applied to a completely new block of the material if preferred). Put the Stemfix, old or new, into a plastic bag with a little water, and fasten the mouth of the bag tightly with an elastic band. Rub the Stemfix and water together, rather as if rubbing fat into flour or pastry. The resulting mixture is like a smooth stiff paste or dough—a little experimenting will soon enable you to get the right consistency.

In this form, Stemfix can be moulded to fit every kind

of container, even the oddest-shaped ones and those which would not otherwise hold sufficient water for the arrangement, and it is ideal for miniature containers. When using, press it very firmly into the container.

How to Use Oasis

The material sold under the trade name of Oasis is similar to Stemfix, but the former absorbs water more rapidly. When fully saturated they are both so heavy that they will hold quite large designs without tilting over. In its block form Oasis is used in the same way as Stemfix, and when the block begins to disintegrate it can be given the plastic bag treatment. Incidentally, in the dough form Stemfix and Oasis can be mixed together.

I keep an ever-ready supply of the dough in a child's plastic bucket. It goes on for years, being used over and over again, and never becomes smelly or unpleasant. When doing a big arrangement, using Stemfix or Oasis in this form, it is a good plan to have a pinholder under the paste at the bottom of the container. This will hold the main stems of the design securely.

Adding More Water

People often ask how extra water is added to an arrangement in Oasis or Stemfix. In the case of the paste, just dribble water slowly on to the surface. If the material is in the block, add water down a hole bored with a knitting needle.

Both Oasis and Stemfix, in paste or solid form, undoubtedly enable flowers and foliage to last for long periods, apparently providing the humidity which they relish so much. This is a marked advantage in the hot conditions of summer flower shows. Topping up with water is rarely required, even at a two-day show, especially when using the paste method. I used Stemfix for an arrangement which had to be left at a photographer's studio after being some time under the strong light for a picture to be taken. For various reasons I was unable to collect it until five days later. The container had been knocked over, but the flowers were all still in place in the paste and quite fresh. I then had the arrangment in my home for four more days.

The Parcel Method

I have often wrapped damp Stemfix or Oasis paste in a sheet of metal cooking foil, forming an attractive-looking parcel which needs no other container. The stems are just pushed through the foil and into the paste. The method can be used in many ways—for instance, to make garlands on the poles of a marquee for a wedding reception, on a newel post at the foot of your staircase at Christmas-time, to decorate the font for a christening or the pulpit and lectern at Harvest Festival.

For a luncheon or dinner party flower arrangement a foil-wrapped parcel can be placed directly on the table without fear of water leaking on to the cloth or the polished wood. A novel table decoration can be made by tying tiny foil parcels to the arms of a silver candelabra to hold red ranunculus and silver-backed grevillea. With candles alight and reflected in the dark wood of the table this makes a memorable decoration. There are countless other ways in which the parcel method can be used; one occasion when I found it especially worthwhile was in decorating a church for a wedding. I arranged flowers in parcels secured to every pew-end right up the aisle.

For Dried Arrangements

Some florists stock a handy material called Florafix, which comes in a soft block. This does not hold water, but it is excellent for arrangements of dried or preserved materials. The block can be cut up into smaller pieces with a sharp bread knife or carver. For amusing Christmas decorations it can be cut into appropriate shapes, such as a snowman or a polar bear, and it can also be bought ready cut in circlets for door swags, indoor wall hangings, and table decorations. Evergreens, colourful fruits, perky ribbon bows, and bright Christmas baubles are all easily positioned in Florafix with short stems made from florist's wire. It will not harm paintwork, wallpaper, or furniture, and being dry and very soft it is pleasant and simple to use.

Invest in Scissors

A good pair of florist's scissors is an investment. These scissors will cut chicken wire as well as thick stems, and cost less than ten shillings. Lightweight secateurs are a good second choice, but kitchen scissors and dressmaking shears are not as suitable as most beginners think and should be avoided.

You wouldn't try to embroider without a sharp needle, or take up gardening without a spade—so treat yourself to the right scissors for flower arranging.

Florist's Wire

Some florists and most ironmongers sell florist's wire in varying thicknesses, and cut into lengths called stub wires. You can push stub wires up the hollow stems of flowers such as lupins to stop them twisting about in an arrangement, or to enable you to bend the stems into graceful curves. Cleverly placed, so that it doesn't show, a stub wire will hold up the head of a weak-stemmed flower. Wiring of flowers, however, is rather looked down upon in the flower arranging world, and is not allowed in competitions if the wire is visible.

In fact, it should not really be necessary to use wire in fresh flower arrangements, though it can be a saviour in an emergency. For instance, if a stem breaks it can some times be repaired by running a wire up the inside to hold the two broken pieces together.

Wire of various thicknesses is needed at the end of the year to make artificial stems for cones, baubles and preserved flowers, for use in Christmas decorations.

Orange Sticks

Orange sticks, as sold for manicure purposes, are excellent as "stems" when using fruit in an arrangement. They will keep apples, pears, etc., in position without harming the fruit too much.

Rubber Bands

I use rubber bands to keep chicken wire secure inside containers. Many people use string for this purpose, but rubber bands are better because they never syphon out water on to the table, as string can do. I like two thick rubber bands, passed right round the wire and the container to form a cross at the top. (*See* fig 7.) The rubber bands effectively prevent the chicken wire slipping about, thus ensuring the vitally important firm foundation on which to build up an arrangement. Believe me, nothing is more infuriating than to complete a beautiful arrangement and then see it fall to pieces because the chicken wire slips.

Nevertheless, when an arrangement is completed and in its chosen position it should be sufficiently well-balanced to stand up for itself, and if the rubber bands are visible they must be snipped with the scissors and gently removed.

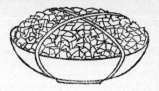

Fig. 7

Buckets Are Necessary

As a flower arranger, you can't have too many buckets! Plastic ones are best, since they never rust or rot, are easily cleaned, and are light to carry even when full of flowers and water. All flowers, leaves and branches should get a long, long drink in a cool place, in a bucket of deep water before being arranged. Sort out the flowers, putting different colours into different buckets. Leaves and other material can go into a separate bucket. This sorting out saves time and trouble when you start the arrangement.

Short-stemmed flowers need something smaller than a household bucket for their deep drink; try a jam jar or a child's seaside bucket. A friend of mine uses a milk bottle carrier, made of lightweight plastic and bought at a chain store, for transporting jam jars full of flowers to shows and exhibitions. Really tiny blooms can be given their pre-arrangement drink in an aspirin bottle **or a** small cream jug.

Florist's Tubes

If you are called upon to do huge arrangements frequently it might be worthwhile to persuade a friendly florist to let you buy some florist's tubes. These are long metal cones which give extra length to stalks and branches.

They can be used as they are, by pushing them into chicken wire, or made even longer by binding them to bamboo canes or strong sticks. They can themselves be filled with chicken wire, and are usually placed right at the back of the arrangement so as to be invisible when the design is completed. As always, the mechanics of the arrangement should remain invisible to the observer!

Raffia and Moss

Thin or very delicate flower and leaf stems (often found in forced spring bulb flowers) sometimes will not stand up in a pinholder. They can be given body by using raffia to bind on a snippet from a thicker stalk.

Moss can play a part in a flower arrangement, either to cover up any chicken wire which is visible when you have finished, or as a planned part of the design. Your florist will sell you a bag of an attractive grey-green moss, called reindeer moss or florist's moss, which is used in wreaths. It comes to the shop compressed and dry, and you will need to soak it for a few minutes in water before using it. After soaking it becomes springy and soft.

In its dry state, however, this moss can make an unusual addition to a small design. I once did a rather pleasant little coffee table arrangement with polished green ivy leaves, grey moss and gold button chrysanthemums arranged like a Victorian posy. Used either dry or wet, reindeer moss seems to last for ever. I keep mine in a small plastic bucket and let it dry out after use.

There are, of course, other mosses to be found in the countryside. You'll discover them in damp spots in woods, ditches, and so on. There's a specially attractive one which grows like a close-clipped green carpet, and others with quite long fronds which you can use like leaves in miniature arrangements.

Transparent Tape

When a curve is desirable in a straight-growing leaf (such as sweet chestnut, aspidistra or a fern frond) run a stub wire up the back vein of the leaf and secure it with a length of transparent adhesive tape. This is best accomplished with the leaf placed flat on the table. When the wire is firmly fixed the leaf can be carefully curved into the required shape. Similarly, preserved leaves can be given long stems by taping on stub wire in the same manner.

I have a poor memory, and once arrived at a flower arrangement show without either a pinholder or chicken wire. I saved the day by sticking pieces of transparent tape in a criss-cross pattern over the container (*see* fig. 8), leaving spaces in between for the flower stems.

Oil Is Useful

A light oil may be used to clean leaves which have been grown in the grimy atmosphere of a town or city garden. Oil will also give additional highlights to very smooth leaves, such as camellia, laurel and rhododendron, for exhibition work. I have seen begonia rex and eucalyptus leaves oiled, but to my mind their characteristic textures are altered in an unpleasing way. Whenever you do oil a leaf, use a bit of soft rag dampened with a very small quantity of oil.

Fig. 8

Stones and Pebbles

Seashore pebbles, worn smooth by the action of the sea, or
well-shaped garden stones are sometimes used in shallow
containers to give an out-of-doors effect. The idea of a
cool waterside scene, for example, is emphasised if flowers,
leaves, and perhaps bulrushes are arranged at one end of a
dish and pebbles scattered where they can be seen through
the water.

The perfectionist will use only water-worn pebbles and
rocks in such a scene, leaving the more rugged shapes of
garden stones for use with ferns and wild flowers in a
arrangement with a wild or woodland flavour. Some of
my favourite pebbles—lovely smooth black ones, flat and
about the size of a florin—were picked up on the beach in
the harbour of St. Ives, Cornwall. I have never come
across anything quite like them on any other beach.

Heavy pebbles and stones can be pressed into service
to give weight and stability to light containers holding
heavy branches and long stems. I find that some modern

metal containers are not so heavy as they look; they can take large arrangements but haven't the weight of metal in them to prevent the disaster of tipping over. The risk is overcome by half filling the container with stones—but remember that this leaves less room for water, so it may be necessary to top up twice a day.

Some pebbles and stones have specially interesting shapes, suggesing birds or beasts or pieces of sculpture, and these can add a touch of fantasy to a flower arrangement when used as its focal point.

Driftwood is Popular

Arrangements combining driftwood with flowers and foliage are very popular, particularly at the bigger shows and exhibitions. Driftwood is the name given to any wood which has been weathered naturally by water, fire, air, or earth. In other words, driftwood may be pale amber pine tree roots, gnarled burls from a fallen elm, twisted knots of ivy stem, a sea pitted branch—anything with an interesting shape, colour, or texture. When used in competitive work, natural driftwood is regarded as *dried* plant material.

Used imaginatively, driftwood can bring a distinctive quality, something all its own, to a design. It can become the focal point, or determine the height and width of an arrangement. No two pieces are alike, so by including driftwood in even the most ordinary container you imbue a design with originality.

Some driftwood will be conveniently shaped so that it stands up by itself. Other pieces will have to be supported with plasticine or putty, while others again will hold up on the pins of a good sized pinholder. A really heavy piece may need to be screwed to a flat length of wood by a handyman, or have a shelf bracket fixed to it to form a leg. The support will, of course, be hidden under the flowers, fruit, or moss of an arrangement.

A word of warning: some driftwood harbours wood-worm, even if you can't see it. To kill infestation, soak the wood in a weak solution of household disinfectant for a few days. A day in a bucket of strong domestic bleach will give the wood a fine weathered appearance, while a wipe over with a rag soaked in wood stain or dark stain shoe polish adds a richer tone.

In the spring, combine a dry wood stump with sprays of young beech foliage, daffodils and moss. Late summer can see the same stump used with shrimp-coloured dahlias and hosta (funkia) leaves. In the autumn, try using the wood with toadstools and trails of blackberry foliage. Winter may see the same chunk of driftwood still doing duty, with dried poppy heads and summer leaves which have been preserved.

Add a Figurine

Figurines can be effectively linked with flowers. A figurine may be of china, wood, or metal, in the form of a bird, animal, fish or human being. When a figurine is used in a flower arrangement it must appear to be happily at home with the container and the flowers. It is a common mistake to include plastic figures, little glass animals and fluffy toys, but these never look right. On the other hand, an Indian horn bird (*see* photograph no. 4) seems to fit in naturally with dried flowers and leaves, and is equally happy in a water scene.

A fragile Dresden lady would be in keeping with small spring blossoms. A bronze dog would look well with heather, gorse, or grasses arranged on a slice of log to suggest rural surroundings. Small Victorian heads, in marble, bronze, or plaster, can be picked up in junk shops now and then and give an old-world charm as the focal point of a design.

Take time to match your flowers and leaves to the colour of your chosen figurine. White, cream, or pastel-hued blooms go best with marble, plaster, and china, while bronze and gold-coloured flowers enhance metal figures.

CHAPTER 4

Choosing Containers

Part of the pleasure of flower arranging to-day is in seeking out containers. A container need not be expensive by any means; quite often the bit of junk picked up for a copper or two becomes the container most in use and cherished.

I know of one woman who will not use her best container—a little metal dish—at flower shows, in case of loss. She loves it more than all her expensive vases and flower holders. It didn't cost much, but being old it is practically irreplaceable.

There's no doubt about it, the old containers are especially fascinating, though many of them were never meant for flowers. An unusual container brings its own charm to an arrangement, and will frequently prove an inspiration in itself to the beginner. Whenever you buy a container, either new or second-hand, the important thing to consider is its basic shape. Has it simplicity, pleasing proportions, and a generally well-balanced appearance? Any fragile lightweight container which looks as though it will fall over as soon as it is filled with flowers must be avoided—it will merely take up valuable space in your store cupboard.

When buying containers choose those which will suit the style of your own home and your personal taste. Even if you have room for only two or three arrangements in the whole of the house you will need more than two or three containers. The low copper bowl which looks so well with a lovely blaze of autumn colour cannot be so attractive for an arrangement of pink apple blossom and violets on a day in spring. When the garden is producing spires of tall gladioli you will need a container which will differ greatly from the kind you will use to display the first shy Christmas roses.

Then, too, the eye tires of seeing the same couple of containers in use year in, year out. Each container tends to look its best with one particular season's flowers or with one kind of design. New ideas are conceived with a change of container, and the container need not be an expensive one, as you will see. It could be one you have made yourself, or an everyday household dish, or cost just a shilling or two from the white elephant stall at the vicarage garden party. The main object of this chapter is to show you what to look out for and how to adapt it for flowers.

Making a Start

Get used to the word container. It simply means a thing which will display flowers to the best visual advantage, and which will usually hold water. The novice's ideas about containers are usually stiff and stereotyped. There are stick-in-the-mud preconceived ideas that flowers go into things called vases, with an occasional venture by the lighthearted to put them into a jug or a tumbler. All this is now changed!

From the Kitchen

You will find that you have many things in your kitchen cupboard, or about the house, which are suitable for flowers once you start to think about them in this light. Plain ash trays, unpatterned soup bowls, gravy boats, pie dishes, souffle dishes, candlesticks, baking tins, Scandin-

43

avian wood fruit rafts, empty wine bottles, a mustard pot
—all can be used for flowers.

A low glass oven dish can look quite different if you
stick a piece of silver cooking foil on the outside of the
glass. Arrange the flowers at one end, so that the silver
shows through the water, and you have a refreshing
decoration for a summer table.

Even a large potato can be used as a container! Cut off
a slice at the bottom, to make a level base, and add a bit
of plastic material to protect the table. Into the potato
you can push the stems of heather or any of the evergreens, which will keep well in the moisture they absorb
from the potato.

Home-made Containers

There are some containers which can be fashioned at home
quite quickly and effectively. It's surprising what you can
do even if, like me, you are not very dexterous. Things
like cocoa tins may be painted with matt paint, or covered
with the sticky-backed plastic material sold for covering
kitchen shelves. Large round toffee tins, obtained from
your local sweet shop, look well when painted or when
covered with cork bark or any plain-coloured textured
fabric. These big tins will take a flower arrangement for
the hearth in summer, and are useful if you are called upon
to provide a big arrangement for, say, a school speech day
platform.

A tall glue pot can be turned into a Japanese-style container simply by wrapping round it a table mat made from
split bamboo or coarse woven straw. An empty beer or
soft drink can is transformed into a tall elegant container
when given a jacket made from pastel-shaded poster card.
And you'd really never guess their humble origins!

44

Containers from Newspaper and Wire

If I want a very special container, of a shape not easily found, I sometimes design my own. This sounds extremely clever but need not be, as you can discover for yourself. During the past few years I have made classic urns, leaf-shaped dishes, troughs, and numerous other shapes. The cost is negligible. Each container takes only three or four hours in all to complete.

Fig. 9

All you need is a piece of half-inch mesh chicken wire, some newspaper sheets, a large carton of Polyfilla, glue-size, paint, and varnish. A flat dish-type container is the easiest sort with which to begin. Cut the chicken wire to the size and approximate shape you have in mind for the container, and turn up the edges to form the sides. (*See* fig. 9.) Line the whole of the inside with newspaper and, having mixed some Polyfilla in an old basin, smooth this over the newspaper and allow to harden. (Mix only a little Polyfilla at a time, as it dries rather quickly and becomes difficult to work.) Reverse the container and cover the whole of the exterior with Polyfilla, so that all the chicken wire is covered. Leave for at least a day until set.

The surface may now be rubbed down with the blunt end of a nail file or a round-ended knife to take off any humps and ridges. To get a smooth finish a final rubbing over with sandpaper or glasspaper is required. A pleasing effect is achieved if the inside of the dish is made smooth and the outside allowed to retain its rough texture. Give the whole thing a coat of glue-size, and when dry paint the container grey, white, duck egg blue, French grey, or what you will. Finally, apply a coat of clear varnish for a really waterproof seal. If you can get marine varnish, so much the better.

Plaster of Paris

I have made similar containers, using plaster of Paris instead of Polyfilla, but it is necessary to work very quickly as the plaster becomes hard and unworkable within a minute or two of mixing. Plaster of Paris also takes longer to dry out. However, it is inexpensive and very easily sanded down to quite fine shapes.

The more complicated kinds of containers, such as urn shapes, may need a fair amount of shaping and finishing work before being painted. For instance, anything with a foot or a stem needs careful filing to get the form absolutely right.

Pieces of " modern sculpture " to support small flower bowls can be made from strong fencing wire bound round with strips of newspaper and covered with Polyfilla or plaster of Paris.

Pilchard Tins

For arrangements where the flowers, leaves or fruits are used so low in the design that the container itself does not show, all that is necessary is something to hold the water and pinholder. Empty shallow tins, such as those in which sardines, pilchards and herrings are sold, or even a small-size catmeat tin, are ideal. The cut edges must be carefully hammered down, and the tin can be painted black, grey, or white so that it will unobtrusively blend with flowers, foliage, etc.

Fig. 10

These tins, which will take a pinholder or chicken wire in the usual way, have many uses and I find them just the thing when arranging flowers on a plate, a flat piece of wood or marble, or behind a figurine, and when using a container which is itself insufficiently deep. Some salmon tins reveal a bright golden-coloured metal when the labels are removed. I use these for Christmas table decorations; they look surprisingly expensive with a candle in the centre and flowers arranged so that the gold gleams through.

Both sardine and salmon tins can be used on top of a candlestick, though they are not so secure as a candle cup, a specially-made metal container which fits on to the top of any candlestick. The makeshift sardine tin has to be stuck to the candlestick with modelling clay or Plasticine, with a couple of stout rubber bands as an extra precaution. (*See* fig. 10.)

Date Boxes

White plastic boxes in which dessert dates are sold are valuable as containers for horizontal table arrangements, and will take surprisingly large designs. They should be filled with Stemfix or Oasis, wire netting, or a pinholder. If you find yourself having to do flower arrangements on the long tables at, say, a wedding reception, when all the containers must be alike, I can recommend date boxes. Incidentally, my flower club finds that when made up with gay arrangements of small spring flowers these boxes sell well at bazaars.

Gaining Experience

So far as containers are concerned it is a good thing to begin the hobby of flower arranging by utilising household utensils and other bits and pieces. But soon you will want to branch out, to try new shapes. After your initial experiments with the pots and pans you will grow quite knowledgeable about what shapes and sizes of containers to use, but when you decide to try something new don't go first to the department store with its rows of ordinary, mass produced pottery containers. Try the local junk shop instead where you should find a wide selection of suitable containers.

I try not to buy containers just for the sake of buying them (though my family and friends will laugh at this statement, for I am a constant collector of more and more containers). The fact is that after a time, even though one buys more containers, one becomes ultra-selective when choosing them. It is silly to duplicate similar shapes unless they are of different materials. To give an example: You may possess a pottery urn, so you don't want another —but don't pass over a bronze or glass urn if one appears in the junk shop. The flower designs which your pottery

48

urn inspires will be quite different from those evoked by a metal or glass one.

A new container is to the flower arranger what a new canvas is to the artist—it stimulates and delights. This is not an expensive hobby, and a second-hand container will probably cost only a fraction of the price an amateur artist will pay for a canvas. And, unlike the canvas, the container can be used with pleasure over and over again.

Inexpensive Finds

Junk shops are my happy hunting ground, for this is where one can buy the unusual for very little outlay. "But you'll never find anything interesting—those shops have been rummaged through and cleaned out of containers years ago," people say.

That just isn't true, you know. You *can* still find bargains, especially if you buy slightly damaged or otherwise imperfect items. A little bit broken off a piece of china doesn't matter so long as it still holds water and has a "good" side.

Worth looking out for are old black lacquered glove boxes, Victorian shell trinket boxes, small figurines (broken arms and similar damage can be repaired with barbola paste), old vegetable dishes, plain white or simply-coloured sauce boats, plated entrée dishes, jugs, salt cellars, bon-bon bowls, pretty cups and saucers, or any decorative metal object. Even things which leak can be given an inner dish or cup for the water.

You can buy all sorts of pots with the lids missing or broken—after all, you don't need the lid for flowers. I once bought for five shillings a fine old Derby tureen which is now one of my most treasured possessions. The lid was missing—and some weeks later I came across it elsewhere in the same shop, and bought it for twopence!

Candlesticks can be turned to good account, whether made of brass, pewter, glass, wood, or pottery, always making the basis of a good design. Tall candlesticks are particularly pleasing, enabling graceful downward-flowing designs to be achieved.

Glass Containers

Glass is rather out of favour with flower arrangers now-adays and is rarely used, but personally I believe the next few years may well see a swing to glass containers, so buy one or two old pieces now while plenty are available inexpensively.

In selecting a glass container, put it to the same stringent test you would apply to pottery or metal. Are its proportions pleasing? Does it have a satisfying shape? Which flowers might be used in it? Although a glass container doesn't need to be of the best crystal or cut-glass it should have an agreeable fineness; cheap, coarse glass never looks right with flowers.

Clear glass containers reveal the chicken wire, stems, and water. A good way round this problem is to line the container with a broad leaf before the pinholder or netting is put in. The lining leaf will last for three or four days before it begins to decay, after which it *must* be changed.

A Place for Victoriana

Keep an eye open for Victorian mantelpiece decorations, such as bronze (or its good imitation) figures of shepherdesses beckoning to their swains, or warriors rushing into battle. They make original flower containers. The figures should not be much more than a foot in height; anything taller is too big for the average modern home when used as a flower container. Bronze figures with one arm held high are speedily fitted up with a flattish plastic or metal dish to hold water; any handyman can glue or solder the dish to the upraised hand. Five minutes with a paintbrush and a tin of gold paint will turn a discoloured figurine into a passable imitation of ormolu.

Old shop fittings sometimes turn up. A pair of old brass scales make twin containers for autumn's bounty of flowers, berries, and fruits. I have a deep copper sugar scoop with a wooden handle, which I dote on when arranged with fruit, berries and bright flowers. The copper kettle has been rather overdone in recent years and is no longer a novelty, but some silver, porcelain or earthenware teapots make equally attractive settings for flowers.

For a Guy Fawkes night design I once arranged rocketing red hot poker flowers, brilliant flame and yellow dahlias, and the swirling "smoke" of old man's beard (wild clematis) seedheads on an ancient iron fire trivet, using the trivet as a base for a hidden dish. After the show for which the design had been made I took it home and, as the weather was mild and we had no coal fire, stood it in the hearth. A favourite arrangement of mine, using similar flowers, is one I often make up with my kitchen griddle (intended for making Scotch pancakes!) as a container.

Flower arrangers often see possibilities in a white elephant which other people would pass over as being quite unsuitable for flowers. I recollect a friend of mine buying a dull brass Victorian dinner gong; I was among those who thought her quite mad until I saw the gong when she had cleaned it and used it as a container, reflecting a lazy curve of crimson nasturtiums in its highly-burnished metal.

Victorian soap dishes left over from the wash-stand sets of long ago were once so popular with flower arrangers that in some districts they fetched prices which would surely have given our grannies the vapours. I recently saw one in an antique shop, marked 12s. 6d.

Hunt Out Antiques

Antique shops differ from junk shops. One expects to pay more, particularly if the desired article is in perfect condition. But it is always worth asking whether they have anything inexpensive yet suitable for flowers.

All these shops get quite a lot of rubbish in the mixed lots they buy at auction sales; they often have to buy a lot of inferior items in order to secure the one perfect piece they really want. In many shops, the bits and pieces go into a special drawer or cupboard which is well worth hunting through for cheap bargains.

In the Tobacco Shops

Tobacconist's shops often carry stocks of articles which could just as well be on sale in the florist's as containers for flowers. I am thinking of ash trays, cigarette and cigar boxes, and metal containers for holding snuff and matches. My local shop has some shallow onyx ash trays of great beauty, and I can imagine them arranged with small designs of flowers and leaves.

Use a Base

Many an arrangement is improved in appearance if placed on a base of some kind. A design which looks top-heavy can be improved by having a base beneath the container. The base may be a suitable teapot stand, an upturned plate, a block of wood (either polished or covered with fabric), a flat piece of stone or marble, a tile, a tray, a child's wooden building brick painted black or some colour to go with the flowers, or even a book with a drape of fabric over it.

For a real miniature arrangement the base may be a small coin (even a threepenny or sixpenny piece), or a button.

A scallop shell, or indeed any kind of shell, can have a second one stuck under it to form a matching base. (*See* fig. 11). Another idea is to cut a piece of thick cardboard into a wavy shape, cover it with glue, and sprinkle it with coarse sand or granulated cork. This cork, incidentally, comes as packing in casks of grapes, and the greengrocer will probably be only too pleased to give you a bagful for nothing.

Fig. 11

I once saw a magnificent base made from an old door mat! It had been standing out in a north-facing porch and had grown a thick felt-green moss all over it, the weave showing faintly through. It was used as a base, in a competition, for an arrangement of brilliantly coloured autumn flowers. The title of the class was "An arrangement for a barbecue supper."

If you have a wooden cheese or bread board this can perfectly well carry an arrangement of late border flowers, grasses, and the full heads of corn, or daffodils in the spring. You only rarely use the board for cheese or bread? Then try staining it with oak floor stain, or polish it up with dark stain shoe polish, and use it with a small bowl standing upon it.

If you can get hold of the marble top from an old washstand you can have it cut up (at a monumental mason's yard) into pieces of different shapes and sizes.

Made from Bamboo

Thin bamboo canes, bound or stuck together, make a base with the appearance of an Oriental raft. I grow pampas grass in my garden, and after it has flowered I cut the stems, which resemble bamboo canes but which take on more subtle colourings. I make them up into a "raft"; it is an ideal base for an arrangement of showy tangerine geraniums, leaves of jade green or sulphur yellow, seed pods of the lily, or anything of strange and unusual shape. One of those small plaster Chinese figurines, sometimes to be found for a shilling or two, looks well when placed on the raft among the flowers, leaves, and fruit as though sailing off to sell them.

Another type of slatted base can be made with thin wooden dowelling, bought at any do-it-yourself shop. Among container bases I have recently admired was a slate-grey one made from two thin flakes of smooth stone and arranged with woodland flowers and branches. At a show not long ago I saw a wooden base coloured with grey shoe cleaner so that it exactly matched the grey of preserved eucalyptus leaves.

Pleasing Reflections

Some flower designs are seen to advantage when placed on a piece of mirror glass. Glaziers will cut coloured and semi-transparent glasses to order. Thick black glass, of the kind usually seen round shop-fronts, is delightful as a base with green, yellow, and pink arrangements.

Copper or brass trays placed beneath autumn-tinted flowerpieces are quite something! Eastern brasses, with their delicate enamels, are even lovelier when the enamel colours are repeated in the flowers.

As you can see, a base must always be chosen with the same care as the flowers and container so that, visually, they all link together contentedly.

Holiday Finds

One of the pleasures incidental to flower arranging is keeping an eye open for containers wherever one happens to be. Holidays in Britain or abroad usually produce locally-made pottery and other ware, while sea shells and those sea-worn stones picked up on holiday beaches can be quickly converted into containers or bases. Broken or leaking shells can be made watertight with one of the fillers, such as Alabastine, or even by painting over with colourless nail varnish.

To make a container from shells, take a piece of cardboard or wood for a base and pile on it a mound of Polyfilla. On top, press a shell which is large enough and deep enough to hold a few small flowers. Before the mound of filler has hardened, press other pretty shells and stones into it as attractively as you can. (*See* fig. 12.)

All flower arrangers enjoy doing baskets of flowers, and nowadays baskets come in every shape and size imaginable, from fruit punnets to bicycle baskets, and they can all be used imaginatively for flowers. Just put a tin or dish inside to hold the water and chicken wire.

Shape Is Important

Some containers are difficult to use because their basic design is so frightful that no one could make anything of them, no matter how skilled. Other objects which one

Fig. 12

finds tricky to begin with can be mastered in time. The *shape* is the important thing; even over-decorated containers can be used, painted in a single unobtrusive colour, so long as their general shape is pleasing.

Miniature Containers

On trying their hand at a miniature arrangement for the first time, many women are surprised to find how clever they can be with the very smallest flowers, leaves, etc. But some container in good proportion to the tiny flowers is the first requirement. Household things like a thimble come to mind; more unusual is an antique patch box; just as charming is the cup of an acorn, stuck to a bit of mossy bark to keep it upright.

I have arranged flowers in a pair of French porcelain shoes measuring under one inch long, and a less exotic but just as original container of which I am fond is a tiny wheelbarrow, constructed by my husband from a kit sold in the chain stores. I stand this little wheelbarrow on a small flat stone, which adds a lovely feeling of outdoors.

At one show I saw a green poppy seedhead, with its centre carefully scooped out, serving as a holder for a miniature posy. But perhaps the most charming miniature container I have had the pleasure of seeing was made from a lichened twig, stuck to a little cardboard base covered with more lichen. In the cleft of the twig was half the shell of a minute blue egg, filled with Stemfix to hold the flower stems.

I know someone who specialises in collecting miniature containers, and her china cabinet displays dolls' china teaware, minute porcelain watering cans, a little silver cup, and a pewter jug only half an inch tall. She has three children who are just as enthusiastic as she, and the four of them take some defeating when it comes to competitions for miniatures at flower shows!

Miniature arrangements sometimes look more effective when standing on a proportionately small base. A mother-of-pearl button, shading pink and dove grey, is one of mine. I stand an aspirin bottle top on it as a container. The button's colouring is, of course, picked up in the flowers I use.

One of those little Corinthian columns, used to divide the tiers of a wedding cake, will make possible a miniature pedestal design. I admired a whole class of these at a Christmas show, and found each entrancing. The very smallest miniature brass candlesticks, costing about four shillings, will make a doll's-house-size pedestal arrangement.

For the petite arrangement (which for competition should measure from four to nine inches) as distinct from the true miniature (not more than four inches), a hollowed-out tablet of toilet soap, filled with moist Stemfix or Oasis, makes a novel container.

From the Shops

In the shops and chain stores there are many good cheap buys—items not actually intended as flower containers. For example, biscuit tins, wire fruit baskets, plastic egg cups, dolls' furniture, inexpensive figurines, and the decorative little boxes sold for holding pills, jewellery, or hair grips. A container of mine which is constantly mistaken for jade is, in fact, a 2s. 11d. bath salts bottle, made of plastic! Just use your imagination, and there are containers galore.

Difficult Containers

Before buying any container, consider carefully what kind of flowers you will arrange in it. Will the design of the container allow the blooms to flow down at the sides and over the front rim or lip? Some shapes make this difficult. Things such as low vases held by cherubs are lovely to look at, but are not always so easy to work with, as the figures invariably get in the way of the flowers. This type of container may best be left to the experienced arranger, but it certainly looks well on anyone's display shelf.

I am very fond of cherub containers, and have quite a few. If possible, the arrangement must be designed in such a way that the figures are not obliterated; this may mean that the whole arrangement must be designed around the cherubs, so that they take their appointed part in it. If there is a single cherub to one side of the container it may be possible to turn the container so that this figure comes at the front. Then the flowers are arranged behind the cherub, making it the focal point of the design (focal point will be explained later in this book). A low container flanked by cherubs or other figures can sometimes take only an informal line arrangement, the flowers passing down between the figures.

Avoid dishes and vases with wavy rims; they tend to syphon water out on to your table top. Some pottery is porous and oozes water, but this can be cured by applying a coat of clear nail varnish or one of the patent water-repellent sealing substances.

Containers on Display

There is tremendous pleasure to be derived from a permanent display of containers which are in themselves beautiful or interesting. Shelves, or an alcove with a concealed light, make a decorative feature in the hall or drawing-room.

Pride of place in my own display is held by a perfect bronze and marble Regency urn which I found, covered with cobwebs, in a dark corner of an antique shop. The proprietor said it had been there for years, even though the shop was a regular haunt of members of the local flower club. I bought it for 15s.! The moral is that you can find containers in the most unlikely places.

CHAPTER 5

Preparing Flowers and Leaves

If you give time and thought to designing and completing a flower arrangement, it is disappointing to find it has only a very short period of charm before it dies. Naturally, flowers die, and this brief life is part of the fascination of our hobby, for there is always the stimulus of new ideas and fresh flowers just around the season's corner.

But, with care and a little know-how, flowers can be persuaded to stay in peak condition for much longer periods.

I found quite early in my study of flowers that not all have the same life expectancy. The time of the year and the weather conditions all affect the life of a cut flower. It is folly to expect an identical performance from all flowers at all times. Some will have a shorter life than others, no matter how much care they receive.

This surprised me at first. In the old days I thought that, given a change of water every day, all flowers had a similar life-span. When they died quickly in my arrangements I usually thought the florist had sold me duds. I had a lot of trouble with garden roses, I remember, and stopped picking them in quantity; I found it too distressing when, as usually happened, they flagged and refused to be resuscitated no matter how zealously I changed the water!

Old Wives' Tales

The flower arranging novice usually finds she is told a

number of old wives' tales—that some flowers and leaves kill others by a slow underwater poisoning (they don't); that changing the water daily is vital to flower health (it isn't; the water stays quite fresh and wholesome so long as all underwater foliage is removed); that aspirins and pennies in the water supply a magic elixir (in my experience, they don't).

In fact, you will find that by their very make-up some flowers just do live longer than others. Tulips will always continue in an arrangement for days longer than daffodils, even if both are equally fresh to begin with. Early hot-house blossoms, which frequently have been forced, do not have the same sturdiness as their later garden counterparts.

Ranunculus stays beautiful in an arrangement for weeks on end, and so do grape hyacinths. Chrysanthemums last better than maybe any other flower we buy or grow. Zinnias, achillea, carnations, spurge, and orchids are all good stayers, and I'm always delighted at the way gladioli go on opening their successive buds, right to the top of the spike.

Remember that flowers having a number of buds on one stem will usually give a longer show of bloom than those which grow singly. Blooms should be cut away as they die. Foliage will nearly always survive longer than flowers, and I cherish a memory of some camellia sprays which I had for three months, in and out of a miscellany of different arrangements.

When you have to buy your material it's obviously important to take special note of subjects with this built-in tendency to longevity. If you have a garden or green-house this is not so important, though one always wants to give an arrangement the longest possible span of life.

When to Pick Flowers

When I am wanting flowers for some special occasion, such as a show, and the forecast ahead is for a couple of wet days, I cut most of the blooms I shall need, in bud, before the rain starts. The cooler air helps them to last well, while the shelter of the house keeps them unmarked by rain.

Leaves love to soak in the rain, and will invariably live a long time if picked during or immediately after a good shower. Grey furry foliage proves the exception to this rule, however; if it once becomes really wet it just goes on looking bedraggled. Most people know that leaves take on richer hues as autumn approaches, but the flower arranger notices that both leaves and flowers in their late summer maturity live longer than they do when picked earlier in the year.

Every plant has a time in its growth when it is at its best for cutting or picking. If you have a favourite flower which has in the past defeated you by flagging when brought indoors, try picking it at a different stage of its development, or a different time of year. To give an example I've heard people say that they cannot get the leaves of hosta (otherwise known as funkia or plantain lily) to stay crisp in an arrangement. The remedy is to pick the foliage when it is not too young.

Similarly, the Lenten hellebore can be a difficult flower to use in early spring, but later in the season, when the petals have become thick and strong, they will last indoors for many weeks. Both hosta and hellebore *can* be picked in early spring, but it is then necessary to be more fussy about conditioning them before arrangement (more about this later).

How to Harvest

Start right at the beginning. If your garden is a large one it is a good idea to carry a bucket or a large jug full of water around the garden with you, so that each flower you cut goes straight into water. Strip off any thorns, and the lower leaves.

My garden is a small one and I like to pick and match the flowers as I go, holding them in my hand and working out a colour scheme. With, say, a spray of pink roses in my hand I wander around the beds and borders, matching up flowers or finding new contrasts. Scientific colour wheels and study of the spectrum, to determine which colour goes with which, are not for me; I prefer to trust to my eye.

When using this method of gathering, remember to put down the majority of your bunch in a cool place as soon as you have decided on your colour scheme. I have one or two shady spots where the flowers come to no harm while I finish picking the remainder of my needs.

Cutting the Stems

Water is taken into the flower or leaf through the cut in the stem where it was severed from the growing plant. When cutting, use sharp scissors or secateurs and make a clean slanting cut across the stem, rather than a straight cut. This is to give the largest possible area of cut stem, thus enabling water to be taken in more easily.

A freshly-cut stem will drink more readily than one which has become dry at the base. So if your flowers have been out of water for very long always make a fresh cut by snipping a bit off the end of the stalk. As you gather garden flowers, or on reaching home with shop-bought blooms, snip away any foliage, thorns, berries, etc., which might come below water level in the finished

Fig. 13

arrangement. Submerged foliage quickly decays and causes the water to become unpleasant. Thorns and bits of stems or side shoots will, if left on, get caught up in the chicken wire and cause needless obstruction when removing dead or wrongly placed flowers from the container.

In the case of large single leaves, which grow in such a way that they have to be cut from the plant without a stem (such as foxglove and polyanthus), some of the leaf is bound to be under water when placed in the arrangement. I overcome this difficulty by removing as much as possible of the lower fleshy part of the leaf, leaving only the broad mid-rib to go into the water; the rib acts like a stalk (*see* fig. 13).

Removing part of the leaf in no way affects its life span, for it goes on drinking through the rib. This method offers another advantage: The rib can be easily threaded through chicken wire or impaled on a pinholder.

Flowers, leaves, and so on with hard, woody stems must be prepared before arranging by slicing the bottom half-inch or so of stem (*see* fig. 14), to allow water to be absorbed. An alternative to slicing is to hammer the end of the stem.

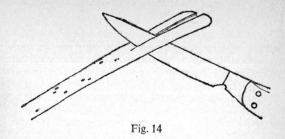

Fig. 14

Choosing Flowers in the Shop

For people with very small gardens, or no garden at all, the florists' shops are invaluable. Florists, I find, will always order the particular flowers I need for a show or a special occasion, and many florists and their assistants take a keen interest in flower arranging, bearing with us patiently when we can't make up our mind whether to take the pink or the red tulips to go with something we already have in the garden. But choosing flowers and foliage from a shop or in the market has more to it than just the question of colour.

Freshness is of paramount importance. If the flowers have been carefully treated by the growers and the shop people they should still be in perfect condition when you get them home—but it is necessary to know how to recognise fresh blooms.

All flowers should *look* as though they have only just been gathered. If they are at all crushed they may never regain that pristine appearance which is so desirable.

Anemones, which are with us through so much of the winter, should be showing true colour when bought. If they are in too-tight bud, and looking pinched with cold, they never open out properly.

Gladioli should have most of their buds waiting to come out, so that you get your money's worth of pleasure from the long-lasting spikes, which open so well in water.

Roses, tulips, poppies and iris are best bought in bud. So are daffodils, for that matter, if you can find them in bud. Bunched tulips and daffodils should squeak when gently shaken. When buying dahlias look at the backs of the blooms—the petals must be crisp and not falling.

All flowers are firm to the touch when fresh, and their leaves will snap easily when bent back between the fingers. Those known for their perfume, such as sweet peas, lilies, stocks, etc., are at their most highly-scented when young.

These are only a few examples, but they serve as a good general guide, especially if you remember that leaves should be firm and unflagging. Any flowers which are normally sold with their leaves (e.g. chrysanthemums) must be treated with suspicion if the foliage has been stripped away.

As the shop assistant takes flowers from the vase in which they are displayed, notice whether the water has any odour of decay. If it has, you will be wise not to buy. Annual chrysanthemums and stocks are particularly susceptible to this simple test.

Judgment comes with experience; you will develop an eye for freshness. If flowers don't look perfect in the shop it is no use believing the explanation that "They'll pick up when you get them home, madam."

Preventing Air Locks

Cut flowers and leaves must have water in which to live. This replaces the life-giving fluids sent up from the growing plant to the flower. Between cutting and getting them into water, however, the stems may develop an air lock—the kind of thing which sometimes prevents the water flowing in household pipes. An air lock prevents water being drawn through the stem, even if the flowers are in deep water, and this is often the chief reason why flowers in an arrangement quickly wilt.

Since we cannot *see* an air lock, it is wise to give all flowers and leaves a precautionary treatment before arranging them. Hot or boiling water will remove an air lock, and the following paragraphs tell how it is done.

The majority of flowers with soft pliable stems (such as red hot pokers, marguerites, etc.) will be fine if given a drink in a jug of *hot water* after picking. Hard-stemmed subjects (e.g. chrysanthemums, buddleia, firethorn, wall-flowers, and phlox) do better with a *boiling water* drink. Stand them in a bucket containing a few inches of water which has just been boiled in a kettle. Incidentally, the steam does not harm the flowers; they actually appear to relish the treatment. Use a plastic bucket; I once ruined a bunch of flowers by putting them into boiling water in a metal bucket without realising that the metal retains the heat far too long for the flowers' comfort and actually causes collapse.

A milk bottle or jug, with hot water from the tap, will do for smaller flowers. When the water has cooled, fill up with lukewarm water and let the flowers drink for a few hours.

Although the *lower* stems of leaves may safely go into very hot or boiling water, the leaf itself must not. There are some plants which have stems that are soft in their young and immature state but which become hard and woody in the older growth (I am thinking of such shrubs as hydrangea, and many of the annual flowers). These will need the boiling water treatment when they are woody, but merely hot water will suffice when they are in the more tender state.

Some difficult subjects require stronger treatment. These include lilac, laburnum, lupins, hellebores, mimosa, delphiniums. Regardless of whether their stems are hard or soft, these must have the *tips* of the stems immersed for about half a minute in a pan of water which is *actually boiling*. To do this, put a few flowers together in a small bunch and protect your hands and the flowerheads with a cloth while you hold the stems in the pan. Another method is to thrust the stem ends through a sheet of tissue paper and gently hold the paper round the blooms while the boiling takes place. (*See* fig. 15.) Yes, I know all this sounds terribly drastic, but it really works wonders, and not least for shop flowers which may have been picked several days before you get them.

First-aid Treatment

Flowers which, though fresh, have begun to wilt—for instance, after being transported by car on a hot day—will speedily recover if placed in a plastic bucket of hot water.

On no account put flowers grown from bulbs (i.e. daffodils, tulips, etc.) into very hot or boiling water—they don't like it at all. Most other flowers, however, have an extended life when given the hot water treatment. In particular, roses thrive on having their stems boiled. Indeed, I would say it is vital to give roses this tonic before arranging them in warm weather.

In all cases it is quite safe to leave the boiled end of the stem untouched, even if it has gone soft, though you can cut it off if you need to shorten the stem when doing the arrangement. It will be found necessary to cut off the

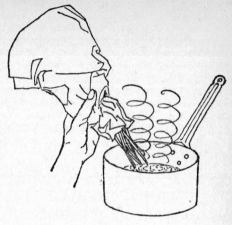

Fig. 15

boiled part, of course, when using a pinholder, in order to gain the required rigidity.

Some flower stems flow with a milky substance when cut (poppies, for example); immersion in boiling water will seal the wound while allowing the flower to take up water.

Any flowers which have had the boiling or hot water treatment will almost at once begin to look strong and perky, and can be arranged in even quite shallow containers. Friends of mine with children find it convenient to gather their flowers in the morning, leave them in water all day, and arrange them when the youngsters are in bed.

Treating Foliage

Leaves of any kind, except the grey furry kinds, should be submerged in water—preferably overnight—before being used in an arrangement. The bath is an obvious place for the soaking if many leaves are required; for smaller numbers (and smaller leaves) a bucket or basin will suffice.

The soaking fully charges the leaves with moisture, making them firm, crisp, and so much easier to arrange, as well as helping them to last three or four times as long. Grey leaves, drooping and floppy types of foliage, and other difficult subjects such as hosta, begonia rex, ferns, and hydrangea foliage must have their stem ends boiled in a saucepan, as described earlier. All but the grey types can afterwards be soaked.

Wild Flowers

Wild flowers do not usually last as long as cultivated varieties when used in an arrangement. They are invariably less robust by nature, and often need extra care right from the moment of picking. If left out of water for very long, or carried home in a hot hand, they droop even before they are arranged. Still, there are ways of dealing with them.

A plastic bag will transport even the most tender countryside flowers, though they may drop a few petals in the bag. A newspaper, used like a florist's wrapping, is another good means of carrying them home, and if you can dampen it so much the better. If neither a plastic bag nor a damp newspaper is available, a large dock leaf or some damp moss wrapped round the stems will keep them cool. As soon as you arrive home, put the flowers in deep lukewarm water and leave them in a cool place for a few hours before arranging them.

Wild flowers can, in fact, be kept for a few days without

coming to harm. My mother recalls how, as a little girl, she arranged a large mixed bunch for a wild flower competition. Then the competition was postponed for a week, but when it was eventually held my mother won it with the same flowers, which had been kept carefully at the back of the cool, dark pantry. Nowadays we could put a plastic bag over the flowers before storing them in a cool place.

Filling the Container

After their pre-arrangement drink in deep water, flowers should always be arranged in *clean* containers. Fill the chosen container with slightly warmed water just before starting to arrange. Never use water which is below the room or air temperature. Really cold water is too much of a shock to the flowers.

It is not necessary to change the water every day. Simply top up each evening, using tepid water (not cold water straight from the tap). The level will be noticeably reduced on the first day after arranging the flowers. Large designs will drink more water than small ones, and warm dry weather or room conditions will lower the level much more speedily than a damp cold atmosphere.

Bulb flowers, which won't put up with hot water, like it best with the chill just taken off. Rosebuds open quickly if their containers are filled with boiling water, and if they are wanted for a special occasion but are slow to open they can be brought on by this method.

A Voyage of Discovery

To-day's flower arrangers have discovered many new things about the care of cut flowers which no one had thought or cared about before. To take up this hobby is like starting on a never-ending flowery voyage of discovery. Some things are learned at home through trial and error, but many tips are exchanged with fellow voyagers.

For instance, in a cold church hall on a wet and blustery day in spring I learned about adding starch to the deep drink water given to tulips before arranging them. This is a precaution against the twisting, bending, and curving that tulips indulge in when arranged. Make up some thick starch in the usual way (it will keep very well in a screw top jar, in the refrigerator). Wrap the tulips firmly together in a newspaper and place them overnight in warm water to which the starch has been added. This method cannot be guaranteed to be a hundred per cent successful, but it certainly helps. I have found it useful, too, with doronicum (leopard's bane), which also has a tendency to twist towards the light.

At the Royal National Rose Show in London one summer I was given another good tip, by a nurseryman whose stand of perfect cut blooms I had admired. "With a knife or scissors scrape away about half an inch from one side of the base of each stem, and the roses will never flop, even in the hottest hall," he said. Since then I have proved that scraping off a little of the outer layer of any hard-stalked flower pays good dividends, particularly in hot weather.

Preserving Berries

Berries stay plump and firmly attached to their sprays for some weeks if a coat of clear nail varnish is brushed over them. Once, early in November, a friend gave me a great branch of beautifully berried holly and a bunch of mistletoe, which I wanted to keep until Christmas. I laid them together on the lawn, in the shelter of a north-facing hedge of forsythia. The sun shone, then the rain came, there were sharp frosts, and a dusting of snow, but the berries stayed firm and the leaves crisp.

Keeping It in Bud

For one reason or another, the flower arranger will sooner or later find herself wanting to keep a flower in bud for a few hours, days or weeks. She may have a wedding or a birthday party a week or two ahead; to-day the garden tulips are in colourful bud but in a fortnight they will be too overblown for use. What can be done?

(1) Lots of flowers can be cut in bud and laid away for a time without dying off or coming into full bloom. Gladioli, chincherinchees, tulips, and early pink double prunus will keep for up to three weeks if each flower or spray is wrapped firmly in tissue and laid flat in a lidded box on a cool floor (for instance, the concrete floor of a garage). Some varieties of rose will last like this, too, if picked in bud, and daffodils will stay in bud, though only for a few days. My favourite florist successfully keeps many flowers in bud by this method.

(2) Buds which you want to keep back for only a few hours or a few days can be retarded by winding a length of knitting or darning wool firmly but gently around them. (*See* fig. 16.)

(3) Another method is to wind strips of tissue round each tight bud and to fasten this with wool. I first saw flowers dealt with in this way when I visited the home of friends a day or two before the big annual show of the British Iris Society. I was intrigued to see buckets of iris with each individual bud swathed in a trim cocoon of tissue held with a rubber band. At the show I took pleasure in helping to untie them. Some buds stayed as they were, in close, tight furls. Others had developed beyond the bud stage, but were retarded, and they slowly unfurled in our

73

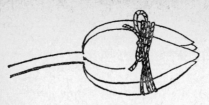

Fig. 16

hands as the tissue was removed. Since that day I have used this trick a good many times to slow down the development of cut blooms.

Temperature plays a part in determining how long a tied flower will contain itself in bud. The flower goes on developing in its tie, and on hot days (or in warm rooms) only the very closest buds will fully retain their tight shape.

Ready for a Show

Any reasonably large flower can be temporarily retarded by the tying method and I regularly use it for poppies, clivia, iris, nerines, gladiolus, daffodils, tulips, and most flowers with pointed buds destined for show or exhibition arrangements. I keep them in the hall (the coolest part of the house) the night before the show.

Anyone who has ever wanted roses for a show will know the maddening habit they have of being past their best a couple of days too soon. They can be held back while still in the garden by having the buds tied loosely with wool and covered with a paper bag.

74

Coaxing Buds into Flowers

At the other extreme, there are times when we need to make flowers open sooner. Perhaps we need them for a show, but the weather is cool and they just won't come out. Sometimes a rose, a double tulip, carnation, or other bloom can be coaxed into breaking bud ahead of its natural time. Pick the bud, stand it in hot water in a warm room, and gently blow into the petals to help them unfold.

Standing the buds under a table lamp will help them on, too. This is sometimes useful when two or three open blooms are required to add visual interest to a very special arrangement. However, if the flower is very immature when coaxed to open early it may never attain its full colour, and will almost certainly produce a smaller bloom than is normal.

One Special Bloom

Tulips can be opened wide by gently smoothing back the petals with warm fingers. Some people hate to see them opened in this way, believing that it spoils the whole character of the flower. Undoubtedly though, tulips have lovely centres, and these are seen only when the flowers open wide in spring sunshine or in a hot room. You may think that two or three wide-open flowers add lustre to a flower design, and this is all a matter of personal choice. Artificially opening the blooms does not harm them or shorten their life.

Early Blossoms

Sprays of pussy willow, japonica, forsythia, fat-budded branches of apple, and the early spring flowering shrubs can all be encouraged to blossom weeks before their normal time. Bring in the bare branches, split the ends well, and stand them in a bucket of boiling water. Place the branches in a good light, or the flowers will not come out quite true to colour. Give hot water drinks occasionally and the buds and leaves will soon expand. Flowering currant, if picked in the early part of the year, left in a dark cupboard, and given hot water drinks from time to time, will be in lovely white blossom when brought into the light in March.

Preserving Foliage

With memories of grandmother's dried pampas grasses, enthusiasm for preserved leaves and flowers is usually sound asleep until the flower arranger opens her eyes to the interesting forms and shapes which can be added to winter designs by means of summer preservation. In fact, during the summer and autumn it is possible to preserve foliage in readiness for the flowerless days ahead.

Beech, oak, and chestnut, as well as foliage from many other trees and garden shrubs, can be preserved quite successfully in a mixture of two parts water to one part glycerine. This mixture need be only two or three inches deep in a bucket; stand the twigs and branches in it until you can see traces of glycerine in the leaves.

I did not have too much success with this system until I discovered that the water should be *boiling* when added to the glycerine; this dissolves the glycerine thoroughly and allows the stems to take up the solution more readily. Stems should be first hammered or sliced at the ends, and should be put into the solution as soon as possible after cutting.

It sometimes happens that a considerable time elapses between gathering foliage and getting it home; in such a case, give the leaves a drink in boiling water before the glycerine mixture. For some reason, leaf sprays occasionally refuse to take the glycerine, so any which begin to shrivel and dry up must be removed and replaced by a fresh-cut stem.

You can't rush the glycerine process, so it may take several weeks for the treatment to become effective and the leaves to turn colour. Glycerined leaves never remain their original colour, but change to rich hues ranging from dark green to rich brown. The colour is largely determined by the time of year at which the leaves are picked.

A member of my flower club always has huge arrangements of these many-coloured preserved leaves standing in the stone-flagged hall of her farmhouse. I have never seen them so variedly colourful as here. The reason is that there are many beech trees nearby and she is able to gather leaves and preserve them at different times throughout the season.

More Material to Preserve

Last year I saw ordinary moorland heather perfectly preserved by the glycerine treatment. The small leaves had turned to a copper colour and this added to the effect rather than detracted, for the heather flowers had retained their own natural colouring.

I have also seen whitebeam leaves which have been given the treatment, and I have myself successfully preserved the fluffy-headed old man's beard. The latter, when required for preservation, should be gathered at any time after the formation of the distinctive green seedheads, before they have turned fluffy. The beard turns a soft ivory shade after absorbing the glycerine, the base of each beard (which is the seed) deepens to a soft brown, and the leaves turn mahogany. These sprays are useful for pedestal arrangements, large or small, in the autumn or at

Christmas time. They may be used just as they are or with the leaves lightly gilded.

The leaves of eucalyptus, iris, montbretia, gladioli, castor oil plant, aspidistra and ivy, and green-podded honesty, can all be preserved with glycerine. Each will add a touch of interest or a note of drama to an out-of-season flower or foliage arrangement.

How to Iron Foliage

A splendid way to keep foliage for winter use is to iron it. This may sound mad, but it really works with many leaves. I have some which are two years old. Pick the leaves on a dry day, and press on both sides with a fairly hot iron. The iron must not be so hot as to char the leaves or scorch them. You need an old cloth to protect your ironing board, but the leaves themselves do not need protection from the iron.

Thick, squashy leaves like those of begonia, cannot be successfully ironed, but most others are suitable. Trails of Virginia creeper, picked and ironed when changing red, are charming. Yellowing bracken, green fern, or tan-coloured sycamore leaves, picked up from where they have fallen, are also ideal.

Some people press leaves between sheets of newspaper under the carpet, but I have never found this method very satisfactory.

Yellowing gladioli foliage makes a useful addition to winter-time decoration when ironed, and any prettily-coloured leaf will retain its colour (or maybe go just a little paler) and still be as usable as when it was alive.

Iron right over each leaf, but try not to break the ribs. After ironing, place the leaves flat under a heavy book or similar weight until all the moisture has dried right out.

These ironed leaves are much more brittle than those preserved by the glycerine process, and so need to be carefully handled.

It is a good idea to do an arrangement of ironed foliage as soon as possible after the leaves have dried out. Put a plastic bag right over the finished arrangement, and keep the whole thing in a dark place until you need it to brighten a room in the winter.

Dried arrangements are not very suitable as all-the-year-round decorations, and should be thrown away (or the ingredients stored flat in boxes) long before spring cleaning time finds the dust lying thick upon them.

Preserving Seedheads

Everyone can get additional pleasure from garden plants by allowing the various seedheads to remain until dried out naturally by wind and sun. These can then be harvested and used in arrangements throughout the winter. Look out specially for poppy seedheads; pick some while they are still grey-green, allow others to go brown, and leave some in place on the plants all winter so that they stand a good chance of becoming skeletonised.

Iris, gladioli, hollyhock, foxglove, candytuft, and many other plants of the herbaceous and annual species give lovely seedheads which dry on the plant or else can be cut and then dried indoors. They can be used in arrangements just as they are, to eke out fresh flowers, or may be painted and glittered for Christmas decorations.

Dried gladioli leaves, and those of laurel, can be made to resemble old tooled leather if lightly brushed over with gold paint. Use them with gilded seedpods in a flowerless arrangement at Christmas.

Gilding the Lily

I am very fond of gilded leaf arrangements for autumn and winter decoration. They look very grand and unusual if arranged in a gilded container. Several different kinds of gilded leaves and seedheads should be included. The effect is not at all garish if the gold paint has been applied sparingly, in touches on leaves and seedheads, rather than covering them all completely. Gold paint can be bought in different tones, from pale to deep, and using several different ones gives a subtle added sparkle to an arrangement.

In the Airing Cupboard

A number of things which at first sight seem useless for arranging can be successfully dried and then put to good use. Pineapple tops are a favourite with me; they dry easily when cut from the fruit and I have had some of mine for four or five years. They make impressive focal points in arrangements, and look especially splendid in wooden containers. I dry them in the airing cupboard, which is usually more taken up with this sort of thing than with laundry on autumn days. The airing cupboard is ideal for drying off material like aspidistra foliage and small sprays of ivy leaves, both of which keep their colour perfectly.

Globe artichokes play an important part in my dried arrangements. To preserve them, stuff pieces of paper between all the "petals" and ease them out into a natural-looking flower shape. Leave them in the airing cupboard for a few weeks, until they are thoroughly dry, then remove the paper. Artichokes done in this way look exactly like carved wood when the drying process is complete, and they make perfect focal points in dried arrangements.

ILLUSTRATED SECTION

O N the following pages there is a selection of photographs showing various flower arrangements. Few of the containers are unusual. Yours may not be exactly the same but don't let that hinder you. You are bound to have odd dishes and containers around the house which are roughly the same shape and size and these will serve the purpose admirably. Always be on the lookout for suitable dishes; junk shops, salerooms and jumble sales can often yield unexpected treasures for the imaginative flower arranger.

The blooms used in these illustrations should be quite easily obtainable in season. Notice that simplicity is the keynote of most of the arrangements and that the best effect is gained by using the minimum of flowers.

CAPTIONS TO PHOTOGRAPHS

1   Early forsythia arranged with hyacinths in a stemmed glass.

2   A lazy curve of camellias, arranged for a coffee table. Any dark leaves can be used as a foil for the flowers. The container is a square glass ashtray.

3   A crescent (or "C" shape) design of snowberries and flowering myrtle in a silver trifle dish.

4   An Indian carved horn bird adds interest in this composition of dried hydrangea blossoms and filigree foliage.

5   This lovely little arrangement of lavender spikes and garden pinks smells as sweet as it looks! Every sort of basket, if given a dish to hold water, makes a very suitable setting for unsophisticated blooms.

6   A composition of little wild daffodils, in two small containers which are hidden by a common fungus (*Polystictus versicolor*). This fungus is often to be found on old tree stumps and logs.

7   Daffodils, narcissi, broom, and Japanese quince arranged with ivy leaves in a reversed "S" shape (or Hogarth Curve).

8   How to start the arrangement shown on the left. Outline stems of the design in place, showing the candle-cup filled with chicken wire.

9   A gilded arrangement for autumn. A dried hydrangea head, globe artichokes, and sweet corn are secured on a pinholder which stands on two wooden table mats.

10 Yellow narcissi, flowering Japanese quince, and orange tulips in an antique container, arranged in a formal triangular shape.

11 First step in a simple but pleasing daffodil design: blobs of plasticine are put on to the underside of a pinholder; these will anchor it firmly in the soup dish which is being used as the container.

12 Three buds of double daffodils, two tall daffodil leaves, and a piece of young peony foliage are placed to form the basic shape of the arrangement.

13 A profile view, taken after the addition of more daffodil blooms and ivy leaves, to show how some flowers and leaves are recessed to give a 3-D effect.

14 Moss covers the pinholder, and the design is completed with the addition of a leaf at the lower left-hand side.

15 In a jewel box lined with green velvet are shrimp-coloured geraniums and roses, deeper-toned dahlias, and buff-coloured grasses.

16 A plated trifle dish holds the first lovely garden flowers of spring. Soft pink hyacinth, deeper pink bergenia, and rosy Japanese quince make a charming design. The lower leaves are grey-green and come from a foxglove plant; the top leaves are from the hyacinth.

17 Three sprays of wild rhododendron arranged in a dish which is contained within a metal fruit basket bought at a chain store.

18 Tobacco flowers in a cheap green-and-white striped plastic beaker make a cool and easy summer design.

19 Pink heather in a white china swan. The heather is placed to follow the shape of the swan and also in such a way as not to obscure the fine curving neck and wing. This simple design has a feeling of elegance, grace, and movement.

20 White flowers bring a feeling of coolness to a room on summer days. A design which is light and airy also adds to the tranquil impression. Here, foxgloves, campanulas, and carnations are arranged in a silver container which reflects the light.

21 In a silver-plated "find" from a junk shop are arranged soft yellow and pink gladioli, yellow and pink carnations, and broad bergeni foliage. In the centre are pink crinum flowers.

22 First steps in the arrangement shown on the left. The first three stems are put in to give the basic triangular outline.

23 Filling in the design. Note how the various stems are kept within the triangle shape which was made with the first three flowers.

24 Decorative cabbage, pink with purple veins, teamed with purple-black privet berries in a long soap dish.

5

6

Corn on the cob (sweet corn), either grown or bought, dries well in the airing cupboard, and like the pineapple tops and dried artichokes may be used as it is or else gilded. Dried millet sprays, as sold in pet shops for feeding cage birds, are also useful material for a dried arrangement. All these dried materials can be packed away out of season, and will last for years.

Hydrangeas Will Keep

Hydrangea flowerheads dry to prefection if the moisture is removed from them quickly. I have even picked them on wet days and still had success in preserving them, contrary to the usual advice on the subject. The flowers should be left on the plant until late summer, when the colouring deepens and the heads begin to feel rather leathery.

Cut them off with a length of stem, and remove the leaves. Then into the airing cupboard for a couple of days, until they feel crisp and crackly. All the natural colouring is perfectly retained. Don't make the mistake of a woman I know; she didn't like the thought of the flowers being thirsty, so she put them in jugs of water in the airing cupboard. Needless to say, the experiment was not a success.

Flowers of delphinium, golden rod, larkspur, achillea and acanthus dry well in small bunches hung upside down in the airing cupboard. Flowers have been dried "on shelves in warm cupboards" for at least 150 years. I have an old book which speaks of flowers being hung in bundles from the rafters, the fire below helping the drying process.

Many late border flowers, arranged in a container and left in a warm place, will dry off by themselves. Late roses and dahlias sometimes do this.

Borax and the Queen's Orchid

Some flowers can be preserved by covering completely with powdered borax, dry sand, or silica gel powder or crystals. For this you need a large dress box and an ample supply of the drying agent. First the bottom of the box is liberally spread with borax and a layer of flowers placed upon it.

Then more powder is sifted over them in such a way that it penetrates into every part of the blossom. Layers of flowers and borax can be built up until the box is full; the top layer, of course, must be borax. The whole thing is then placed in the airing cupboard and left until the flowers have completely dried. An orchid which was part of the Queen's wedding bouquet was afterwards carefully preserved in borax—surely the most famous flower ever to have been kept like this.

Chinese Lanterns

The familiar orange-coloured Chinese lantern flowers, which are easily bought in most towns even if you don't grow them yourself, can be hung in bunches to dry. They become much more interesting if, before hanging them, you cut the outer part of the seedhead into four or five "petals," so exposing the green and orange fruits hidden within. Arranged in early autumn with such things as tangerine-hued montbretia, sprays of wine-red berberis foliage and small apples, they look wonderful.

Cut stems of wild dock, in both its green and red-brown states, can be hung upside down in the airing cupboard to dry, and used with chrysanthemums in the dark months. Wild and cultivated grasses have always been arranged with flowers by British women, and when picked will last all winter through.

I have a leaning towards the "natural look" in my garden, and so I leave some tall-growing plants unstaked and untied to soften the shape of the borders and beds. These, picked when gone to seed, provide delightful swerving, swirling, spiral shapes to add liveliness to arrangements of preserved flowers and leaves.

Fresh and Dried Mixtures

I often use dried leaves and seedheads side by side with fresh flowers and leaves. In autumn and late summer the two go harmoniously together, though I don't care to see dried material arranged in conjunction with the fresh flowers of spring and early summer. This is just a matter of personal preference, and you may feel differently.

As in all aspects of flower arranging, the best way is to try for yourself and judge for yourself. Don't be afraid to experiment—the dried and preserved materials offer plenty of scope.

CHAPTER 6

Making a Design

If you are icing a birthday cake, embroidering a cushion cover, or decorating a room you need to have a design in mind before starting the job. With a mental picture of the pattern, shape and colour scheme, icing sugars are mixed, silks chosen, or wallpapers bought. It's just the same with flower arranging.

Try to keep the finished design in your mind's eye while choosing the container, flowers, leaves, etc. In this way you are less likely to pick or buy too many flowers, and when you do the arrangement your hand is quicker and surer. In other words, know what you want to do—and do it!

The Basic Principles

Most people have the gift of being able to picture things in their heads, and when properly cultivated this faculty can be one of the most valuable things in the flower arranger's equipment. When we arrange ornaments on a shelf, or carefully place the ingredients of a salad to look attractive in the bowl, we are simply using our built-in talent for design. The finished effect depends upon whether the design we had in mind was good or bad.

Well, what makes a good design? Whether it is a piece of furniture, a skyscraper, or a flower arrangement the basic principles are the same:

(1) Proportion—the relationship of length, breadth and height to each other. (2) Balance—a good design will not

only look right but will be practical and will not topple over through being lop-sided or top-heavy. (3) Colour— some colours go well together, others clash. (4) Suitability —is the design suitable for its purpose? (5) Visual interest —the colours, shapes and the materials used must all harmonise into a whole which is pleasing and satisfying to the eye.

These, then, are the principles of good design, and in flower arranging they can be sub-divided many times. Yet flower arranging is an art, so there can be few hard and fast rules.

No Need to Worry

There are rules in painting, but gifted artists can break them and produce masterpieces. The same is true in flower arranging, and so the most anyone can do is teach you the essentials. The more fully you master these basic principles, the more you will be able to branch out and the more you will enjoy the hobby.

So many beginners worry about design, but really there's no need. Let's do a simple experiment.

Begin by picking three flowers—a bud, a perfect fully opened bloom, and one with partly opened petals. Add a few well-shaped leaves, and in your hand you hold the ingredients of a flower arrangement. First, look at each flower and leaf for a minute or two. Each will have its best and most beautiful side, each will be more interesting when seen from one angle than from another. Whenever you do a flower arrangement, no matter how small or how large it is to be, try to find time to really look at each piece of material before putting it into position.

For instance, the bud may be a perfect rosebud, a rose in embryo. It may be elegantly pointed, with perhaps a slight curve in its stalk, and it is these qualities in that particular bud which one should try to make the most of.

Place the bud in position in the container, where its silhouette will be seen against the wall; i.e. on the outside of the arrangement, not hidden towards the centre where its shape would not be seen at its best. If the bud has some flaw, like one imperfect petal, position it in the design so that the imperfection is not seen. Then, perhaps, the curve of the stem could be accentuated if a few leaves were removed, or dramatised and shown to better effect by more careful placement of the rest of the material. The idea for a complete design could be inspired by studying that one bud.

The Focal Point

A nearly full-blown rose, just showing its heart, cries out to be placed right in the middle of the arrangement, where its fullness and beauty can be immediately seen and admired. Every arrangement must have such a centre of interest which irresistibly draws the eye; this is called the *focal point*. This is also the centre of balance, and from it everything else should appear to spring. To heighten the visual impact of the focal point flower, surround it with a few leaves, which provide a foil and set off the bloom to perfection.

The half-opened rose from your three should be placed somewhere between the focal point and the bud, so that the three are linked and at the same time form an interesting pattern.

So, when picking flowers, always take some in bud, some partly opened, and at least one in full bloom, and use these in the manner I have described—buds towards the outside edges of the arrangement, the focal point in the centre, and semi-opened flowers filling in between, together with leaves to act as a foil to the flowers and to help make the overall shape of the design.

Making the Outline

Every arrangement of flowers must have a clear-cut outline shape, or silhouette. When I first took up the hobby I was a long time in grasping this point about outline shape. I argued that by arranging flowers to fit in with some laid-down shape all individuality would be lost. I was talking through my hat!

Drop some three or four flowers haphazardly into a vase and they will assume some sort of outline shape. But the shape will be accidental, so it is not likely to be very interesting or pleasing. Now move the flowers around. The outline shape is being determined by you. The accumulated experience of countless flower arrangers through the years has proved that there are a number of basic shapes which are always pleasing.

As confidence and knowledge increase, you can perform many variations on these fundamental themes. Try to decide what shape you want before you begin the arrangement. The shape must always be determined by your material; work *with* your flowers and leaves, never try to impose unnatural formations on them.

The outlines, or silhouettes, of arrangements are usually made with buds or with flowers which are pointed in shape, such as gladioli, flowering dock, larkspur, red hot poker, golden rod, snapdragon. Light colours are usually better than dark for outlines, leafy branches and spear-shaped foliage (e.g. arum, iris, montbretia and hosta) are generally used. Also useful for making outlines are any fine, delicately-shaped things such as wheat, grasses, stems of winter jasmine, and so on.

When putting your outline stems into position, try to

make sure that the spaces between them are of pleasing proportions. Aim at an airy, well-balanced silhouette.

Tallest Stem First

In all types of arrangement the tallest or topmost stem is best placed in position first. It is usually the only one which is perpendicular; all other stems should be positioned at different angles. When this tallest stem has a curve, the tip of the curve should be immediately above the place where the focal point flower will eventually be placed; that is, over the centre lower front.

Every component of the arrangement should tend to draw the eye to the focal point, which is the heart of the arrangement. As you proceed, cut each stem a little shorter than the last, working inward from the outline to the focal point. It follows that the shortest stems will be those of the heaviest and most important blooms, used low down and in the centre of the design. (*See* fig. 17.)

Deep Colours in the Centre

At the focal point you can safely position the deepest colours, the largest flowers, the most interesting leaves. To the eye, these are the heaviest things in the arrangement, and by placing this visual weight in this position you automatically give a feeling of balance and stability to the design. In other words, you avoid that top-heavy look. An arrangement must never look as though it is about to fall over. If it *looks* well-balanced it usually *is* well-balanced.

Filling in the Design

Still keeping in mind the idea of the three kinds of material (bud, full flowers and semi-open blooms), fill in the design between the outline shape and the focal point. Use partly-

Fig. 17

open flowers, more leaves, and colours and shapes which help link up the focal point with the outline silhouette in an attractive way. With practice, all this becomes quite automatic—you start to place the material where it will look best, almost without thinking.

The Principal Shapes

The principal basic shapes are as follows:

> The triangle;
> The assymetrical triangle;
> The S shape (sometimes called the Hogarth Curve or the Line of Beauty);
> The C shape (or crescent);
> The fan (or horizontal) shape;
> The flame or torch (vertical) shape.

It is perhaps appropriate here to deal with a point which often puzzles beginners, the difference between various kinds of arrangements.

Abstract and Modern Arrangements

A modern arrangement is a restrained design in which the arranger generally uses the minimum of flowers, leaves, etc., and attempts to present the plant material in new ways so that the various shapes and textures produce an added impact. Arrangers often gain fresh inspiration for true abstract designs from modern painters who are attempting similar visual impact through their own medium.

Ultra-modern containers call for this kind of design, and some arrangers join art school pottery classes so that they can make their own. Abstract designs are well suited to the modern home furnished with light angular furniture, bright colours and modern paintings on the wall. Another good type of container is a slice of wood which can be stained and polished so that it blends with the furniture in the room and looks attractive. However, these arrangements go with any sophisticated form of furnishing, antique or modern and look most effective with an Oriental-style decor. Generally speaking, the country cottage style of furnishing and decoration is a less suitable setting for a really abstract arrangement.

As the flowers and leaves are few in number, each must be placed with particular care. Each must take its part in the development of the design. Thus, modern designs can be used to show off to advantage a few choice flowers or a few simple blooms. When flowers are scarce, a modern abstract arrangement makes a few look impressive.

In the best modern abstract arrangements every detail of the material plays a part in the design—the tilt of a petal, the lines of a leaf, the twist of a stem are used so effectively as part of the design that the visual impression of them is heightened. Looking at such an arrangements, one might be seeing all flowers, leaves and stems clearly and revealingly for the very first time. When this feeling occurs you have undoubtedly created a work of art.

Mass Arrangements

A mass arrangement presents the eye with a fullness of shape, instead of the strongly linear emphasis of the modern arrangement. Material is used in greater abundance, and many rich and varied effects can be achieved. A modern abstract arrangement usually has flowers of only one or two kinds, but the "mass" can employ the mixed bunches so beloved by British women.

The mass style fits happily with the decor of all homes, except perhaps the most strikingly ultra-modern. Depending upon the choice of container, it can slip contentedly in with fine antique furniture or complement the contemporary furnishings of to-day. When decorating churches, large halls, or rooms, for public functions the mass arrangement really comes into its own, for it is colourful, eye-catching, and understood by all.

Mass arrangements can be quite sophisticated or perfectly homely and simple. As with abstract designs, you can take advantage of the subtle personalities of flowers and leaves, their textures, shapes, and colours, to build up beautiful and satisfying designs.

I believe all flower arrangers can become proficient in both modern and mass arrangements, succeeding equally well with each.

Other Styles of Arrangement

Between the two extremes of the mass arrangement and the modern abstract lie a number of other styles. There is the Landscape, in which the arranger creates a small scene, using suitable accessories and plant material on a

91

base of some kind. Great care should be taken not to overdo the accessories, or the effect becomes fussy and akin to the plate gardens which children make.

A Contemporary arrangement is one designed to fit a present-day home, while a Period arrangement contrasts with the Contemporary, being designed to suggest the feeling of a past age.

Now let us look more closely at the basic shapes which I mentioned briefly earlier in this chapter.

The Triangle

The basic triangle shape is understandably popular with flower arrangers. To begin with, a triangle is a form which is satisfying to the eye. Its firm base lines give security and balance, and it can never be top-heavy. (*See* fig. 18.)

The first step in making a triangle arrangement is to establish the height. This is done by cutting a tall branch or stem approximately one-and-a-half times the height of the container. If, however, the container is a very shallow bowl or dish, the tallest stem should be one-and-a-half times the width of the container.

The quickest way to get the measurement is to hold the stem against the container and then cut it to size.

This rule is, though, only a rough guide for the beginner. As the flower arranger progresses she will find that interesting effects can be obtained by varying the height of the main stem. The importance of the rule to the novice is that it ensures the arrangement will have good proportions.

Having cut the tallest stem, place it in position towards the back of the container, in the centre. Even if the stem is curved its tip should be directly over the focal point. Next put in place two side stems, low down. These

Fig. 18

should be cut to the same length as each other. Place them so that one comes out towards your left shoulder, the other to your right. Now put in your focal point flower, and then go on to fill in with other flowers and leaves, keeping everything within the triangle shape formed by the first three stems. The joy of the triangle shape is that it is so simple but always effective—and yet, because all flowers and leaves are different, no two triangle arrangements will ever be exactly the same.

The Assymetrical Triangle

Yes, this sounds terrifying, but it's really quite simple. It simply means a triangle with sides of irregular length, instead of matching. Think of an ordinary triangle, made up of a base and two sides of equal length, and then imagine it pushed out of shape to one side or the other.

Get a bit of paper and a pencil and draw a few of these irregular triangles—you'll soon see how many variations there are. But, because of that firm outline, they all re-

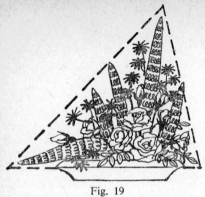

Fig. 19

main well-balanced and pleasing to the eye. (*See* fig. 19.)

It's an odd thing, but some people always make a left-handed assymetrical triangle (that is, with the longest side on the left), while others do it the opposite way round.

On starting the arrangement proceed as for the ordinary triangle, cutting the tallest stem first and placing it in the container. Now comes the difference: The two lower stems must be of different lengths. The lengths will be determined by the proportions of the triangle you have in mind.

The Hogarth Curve
The Hogarth Curve, or S shape, is named after the great 18th century painter William Hogarth. In 1745 he painted a portrait of himself and his dog, now in the Tate Gallery, and included in it his palette with an S-curve painted upon

94

Fig. 20

it and the words "The Line of Beauty." (*See* fig 20.)
Flower arrangers everywhere agree with his definition,
and the Hogarth Curve is a very popular shape. To
achieve this rhythmic "S" you need curving stems and
a tall container, allowing the lower curve of the "S" to
flow down below the rim line of the container.

As in all designs, the tallest stem (which establishes the
height) is positioned first, curving away upwards. Then,
in goes the lower curve, pressed firmly home into the

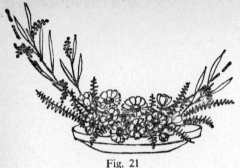

Fig. 21

chicken wire. Make sure that the end of the stem is in water.

It is helpful to have an inch or so of chicken wire above the rim of the container. Better still, use Stemfix or Oasis, brought high over the rim.

The Crescent Shape

The C, or crescent, shape is most useful when you are using material with very curved stems. Once again, make the outline shape first, like a crescent moon slightly over on its back. It can be either left-handed or right-handed.

Then put in the focal point as usual, and fill in with more flowers and leaves. (*See* fig. 21). Make a point of retaining the empty, hollow part of the crescent shape. As with the S shape, the empty space is as important as the shape itself. For the crescent, you may find that you have to trim up branches and leaves, and cut stems quite a lot, to achieve the scooped out look. The crescent design must always look well-tailored.

Fig. 22

The Fan Shape

The fan (or horizontal) shape is a lovely low, restful form, much used for dining table centrepieces and for placing on top of a low bookcase, a mantelpiece, or a window ledge. As the name implies, the shape resembles that of a fully-opened lady's fan, and when arranged for a position where it will be seen from all sides, it should look pretty from every angle.

In this design the topmost stem must be shorter than the two side stems. (*See* fig. 22.) Long, low containers, of oval or oblong shape, are generally used for this design.

The Torch Shape

When space is limited, an arrangement which stresses the vertical line, like the soaring grace of a tall church spire or a flaming torch, is most effective. (*See* fig. 23.)

All the naturally tall and spiky flowers, such as gladioli,

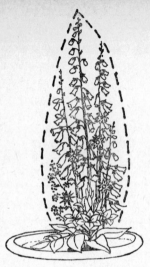

Fig. 23

larkspur, hollyhock and delphinium, lend themselves ideally, for the basic shape of the arrangement repeats their own manner of growth. Bulrushes, iris leaves and tall grasses come to mind, too, for these again will emphasise the upright line. To prevent any appearance of top-heaviness, use rounder leaves and flowers at rim level.

A Frontal Arrangement

The term frontal arrangement is applied to a design intended to be seen directly from the front; for instance,

98

an arrangement to be placed on a side table, desk, or mantelpiece. Because the back is to the wall, a frontal arrangement is very economical of flowers—none need be placed at the back, where they wouldn't be seen. An important point to remember is to put in the main upright stem towards the back of the container. If this stem is placed too near the front you will find yourself with an arrangement which looks as though it is falling over frontwards—and which probably will!

Even though this is called a frontal arrangement, it will be seen also from other angles as people move about the room, and this must be borne in mind as you put in your material. Allow a few leaves to flow back towards the wall to avoid a hard sheared-off appearance.

The All-round Arrangement

This explains itself—it's just an arrangement intended to be seen from any angle. It has its place on dining tables, coffee tables and so on, and should also be used when the arrangement is to be seen reflected in a mirror or against an uncurtained window after dark.

The main upright stem must be placed right in the centre of the container, so that there is room for the rest of the flowers and leaves to be positioned all round it.

Using Curved Stems

To make the swirling patterns of the Hogarth Curve and the crescent moon design, as well as to give a sense of rhythm and movement to other designs, well-curved stems are required. Some leaves and flowers have natural curves, others can be shaped by hand after picking. Even strong twigs and branches can be encouraged into curves by putting the thumbs under a bud or joint

99

and gently pressing down on either side of it. (*See* fig. 24.)

Seek out Nature's beautiful curves. Study each branch before cutting it from bush or tree, and look at the stalk of each flower before picking. Apart from helping you to select the best and most pleasing pieces of material, this will also help to reduce waste.

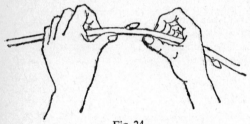

Fig. 24

Broom is a favourite with many arrangers, for it makes a good, sweeping outline and is quickly and easily coaxed into a shapely spiral in the warmth of the hand. Loosely wind the pliable stems round the left hand, as though winding wool, and allow to remain there for a few minutes. When removed, the stems will have a gentle curve, which stays in.

All flowers with fairly long and supple stems can be moulded (gently does it!) in the hand to take on any desired curve. Simply stroke the stem between the thumb and first finger of one hand. The movement must be long, slow and easy, or the stem may snap.

A curving line can also be induced by placing a stem in the chicken wire with the palm of the hand facing downwards and the thumb supporting the stalk. As the stem goes into place, bear down upon it (but gently!) with the warm palm.

Wild Flowers

Wild flowers should never be arranged in over-elaborate designs. Simple arrangements, to match the unsophisticated charm of the flowers, are called for.

The smaller wild flowers, such as primroses, violets, wild anemones, and the little field daisies, will sparkle for days in shallow moss-filled containers, which provide them with the slight humidity they seem to appreciate.

Miniature Arrangements

Miniature arrangements are irresistible, and I am seldom without one in my home. And what popular exhibits they are at shows! Women find them fascinating to look at, but most people fancy that they are too finicky to attempt. In fact, they look more difficult than they are, so do have a go—bearing in mind that a few flowers are better than a lot. Incidentally, some people use tweezers or forceps to put each tiny piece of material in place, and you may find this helpful, though to me it is like weeding in gloves, and I have never found it necessary.

For miniatures, a clear-cut design is vital, and flowers and foliage must be carefully selected to remain in scale with the container. You can't just put big flowers into a tiny container and call it a miniature arrangement. Use this simple test: Imagine the arrangement photographed and enlarged. No matter how big the enlargement is made, every bloom and every piece of foliage should still be in perfect proportion.

How small should a miniature be? Well, the generally accepted definition is anything under four inches, but I

101

have found it perfectly possible to attain a tiny arrangement of under two inches.

What is Recession?

In all flower arrangements, large and small, recession is of vital importance. It sounds highly technical, but it only means that the face of the arrangement should have depth as well as width and height. Or, to put it another way, it should be like a 3-D picture not a flat photograph. This effect is achieved quite easily by cutting some stems short and pushing them well in among the other material. The result is a feeling of depth, added interest for the eye, and a quality of life and movement.

The newcomer to the hobby finds it difficult as a rule to appreciate that flowers can be made to flow not only upwards, forwards, and sideways but also inwards. The focal point is often seen at its best when the flower or group of flowers of which it is composed is pushed a little farther in than the surrounding blooms.

Except sometimes in modern designs, never place flowers so that their heads are at precisely the same level, like a row of soldiers, nor put them in line one above another. Though every bloom is put in *deliberately*, the finished effect is generally more pleasing if it appears casual, rather than stiff and regimented.

Finding the Faults

Each part of an arrangement must look exactly *right*. Each flower and leaf must fit in happily with the whole. Be a perfectionist, and don't leave in anything with which you are not completely satisfied. If a thing looks wrong when you put it in, it will still look wrong when the arrangement is completed.

Look at your finished work through a handbag mirror, or through half-closed eyes. Either of these methods (used by artists when looking at their pictures) will generally show up any fault in the design.

Frequently, some apparently minor detail will spoil an otherwise good arrangement. For instance, the whole appearance can be ruined by one stem crossing the line of another above water level unless this is a planned part of the design. For example, in modern or contemporary arrangements (rarely in traditional ones) stems are sometimes deliberately criss-crossed to form a pleasing pattern. Stems may cross each other under water, but they should never do so where they can be seen.

If you have to change the position of a stem after the arrangement is completed it is unwise to try to pull it out—you may pull others out with it. Cut it off instead.

The Right Feeling

Aim at a feeling of life and rhythm in all your flower designs. A stiff, formal, or set appearance is tedious and lifeless. You can help capture the right feeling by using flowers and leaves of different (rather than matching) sizes.

CHAPTER 7

All About Colour

The colour in flowers can be a lifetime's inspiration to the artistic instinct hidden away in each one of us. Yet people write to me from all over the country to say "But I never seem to have any new ideas for my arrangements—how do you think of colour schemes?"

The answer is simple: I look at flowers.

Do you know the rose Josephine Bruce? I have a bloom of it before me as I write. Here, in this one flower, are a dozen or more shades of colour which can be seen when one studies it carefully.

In bud, it is nearly black. At its most beautiful stage, when the outer petals begin to unfurl, it assumes the red-black richness of old velvet, with plum-red highlights. As the flower unfolds the gold stamens are seen. The new leaves, to my eye, have a lime green tint. This is my favourite red rose.

I arranged it once at the Royal National Rose Society's big annual show in London. The class was for an arrangement of seven blooms with their own foliage, drapes allowed. I used Josephine Bruce, choosing my flowers in various stages of development, from bud to fully opened bloom. I decided on an antique brass candlestick in which to arrange them, and this picked up the stamen colour exactly. My drape was just a little paler than the foliage. Perfect colour harmony was achieved and I won a first.

This is one way to build up a colour scheme with only

one variety of flower. An arrangement of fruit can be handled similarly. Just think of a peach; its green-yellow skin flushes orange-pink and then to deep rose. Now consider it when arranged with not-quite-ripe lemons, yellow plums, green pears, and apples streaked with pink. Visualise it lying on a ribbed and yellowing leaf from a garden cabbage (this, too, blushes pink sometimes) and peach and leaf complement each other in both colour and texture.

I love to experiment with this placing of colour on colour, texture on interesting texture. How absolutely right acid-yellow lemons look on shining dark green laurel leaves, or pale pink roses on wine-red beetroot foliage. Try them!

Mixed Arrangements

In working out the colours of good mixed flower arrangements the same rules apply. Decide, when you walk round the florist's shop or your garden, what is to be the focal point of your arrangement. It may be, say, pink hydrangea flowerheads; most pink hydrangeas tend to be blue-pink, so you can successfully use soft blue, blue-pink, or even blue-red flowers with them. Larkspur, foxgloves, delphiniums, and roses come to mind. The immature hydrangea flowers are often a thick creamy colour, so cream flowers of other kinds will look well in the arrangement.

An autumn arrangement conceived around deep golden heleniums with brown centres might have gaillardias, sunny-toned snapdragons, orange-yellow zinnias or dahlias, fiery red hot pokers, warm chrysanthemums, and shoe-polish-brown iris seedheads, as well as browning dock spikes to emphasise and link up with the centres of the heleniums.

It is how you see and interpret the range of colours in a

single flower which can lead you to a perfectly blended mixture. Even the colour of the stamens can be echoed in the container, leaves, or other flowers.

Only a Few Flowers

If, like me, you have only a small garden, with lots of different varieties of plants, it is usually impossible to go out and pick, say, two dozen pink roses for a large arrangement, so a good effect has to come from nearly as many different mixed flowers.

This is, in fact, a blessing in disguise, for in time you develop a special skill in blending diverse shapes and colours. When this is successfully achieved the finished effect looks far more accomplished (as, indeed, it is) than the carefully arranged dozen of all one kind and colour.

Blend Colours Gently

When arranging a mixed bunch of flowers try not to include too many. Allow the various colours to flow together gently, with no hard edges, rather in the way you blend rouge into your skin colouring. Let the different tones and hues come together delicately, not harshly, so that the whole thing looks subtly planned, not as though it has come together by chance.

This technique of colour blending is difficult to put into words, for a great deal of it depends on personal preference. Some folk hate pink, others dislike white flowers, and so on, but I feel it is well to try to break down one's prejudices, and to keep trying something new. I used to dislike what I call "autumn tints," but I now quite like them after having made myself work with them. So much so that someone said to me the other day "I always associate your arrangements with warm orange and peach colours."

Which shows just how far these exercises in flower arrangement can take you, for these colours certainly wouldn't fit in with any of the decorations in my home.

Not all flowers marry happily from the colour point of view. This is true even in the garden. I was talking once to the head gardener of a "great house" which was open to the public for a day. He and I soon began to talk of flowers and their colours. He interested me by saying "If two flower colours clash in the border I usually find that one or both is a modern hybrid. The old roses, the common wild flowers, and the older varieties of garden flowers always blend well together."

I have found that this truth often applies in flower arranging. The traditional cottage-garden flowers are generally softer in colour, both in leaf and blossom, their shades, tints, and hues quietly blending with each other no matter how mixed a bunch you pick.

Colour Is Exciting

Colour is such an important and delightful part of doing the flowers that it's worth spending a bit of time to get it as near perfect as possible. You can lift your arrangements right out of the rut by applying colour in an exciting way. Use it softly to convey mood, perhaps a cool impression with white and yellow daisies on dark polished wood for an overwhelmingly hot day. Orange-coloured berries, golden roses, or rich flame-coloured carnations bring something of their warmth to a dark autumn day.

With imagination you can almost make flowers speak to an observant audience. Talk about your arrangements to people who come into your home. Women in particular will find it fascinating to discuss exactly what effect you intended with a certain arrangement, and indirectly you may learn something new.

Of course, as you practise and get a sure touch in blending flowers you become better able to put colourful opposites together without discord. Some people find a colour wheel useful. This is a device which shows at a glance the colours that complement each other and those which are opposites. It is a scientific approach which leaves me cold; however, those who would like to experiment with it might get a book on painting in oils or water colours from the public library, since many such books include colour wheels.

Don't Forget Foliage

Foliage may be merely a background for flowers, or it can take a place of equal importance with them. When arranged on their own, leaves can be used exactly like flowers—colourfully. Pick leaves of any shade, tint, or hue that you please, and work them up into a colour harmony. When you really *look* at leaves, in the garden or in the countryside, you will be amazed at the rich variety of colour not only between one leaf and another but at different times of the year.

Use leaves with every arrangement, no matter what it is. Every flower needs foliage for a foil, and arrangements without leaves are strangely bare and unfinished.

Indoor plants, often grown mainly or only for their spectacular foliage, give us leaves which are real treasures in producing varied and striking effects. They introduce colours and shapes not usually found in garden or hedgerow foliage, and are especially useful in the winter. (For more information on this subject, see *Indoor Plants* by Leslie Johns in *Collins Nutshell* series.)

Flower arrangers are often heard to say that they would rather be short of flowers than leaves, so high a value is placed on foliage. I once heard Constance Spry describe leaves as "zones of quiet among the flowers"—an apt description.

Always Something To Learn

One goes on learning about colour. It is never static. Some seasons bring different leaf colours, for example. I have seen my pink hydrangea turn its leaves mahogany red very early in a dry summer, sometimes even while the flower bracts were still in their immature blush-cream tint. Then I have cut both flowers and leaves and used them together, and people have asked me the name of the foliage! It's always fun to be able to add a touch of the unexpected to an arrangement.

As children we learn that leaves are green, except in the autumn, and some people go on believing this. Not the flower arranger; her senses are alert to those "green" leaves which in reality include yellow, near-blue, grey, tan, dull red, and so on. With all these colours in her palette, she can paint pictures which leave the less observant full of amazement.

It's worth remembering that the young growth of early spring produces leaves which are paler in tone than later in the summer. Some young foliage, on the other hand (as from an oak tree which has been lopped), is as gay and colourful as bunting. All kinds of trees and shrubs throw occasional sprays of leaves which are quite out of character with the rest. From a variegated holly tree, to give an example, you will sometimes get odd sprigs in which the leaves are a magnificent splash of delicate yellow.

Looking around my local nursery I found in one of the greenhouses a bit which had been broken off a grey-green succulent. I bought it for sixpence. It pleased me because it showed just a trace of pink in one part. I was able to make it take root, and as it grew the soft creamy pink

developed and took over the green completely. I now have
a most unusual plant which I shall use sometime when I
need just that colour for a special arrangement. (After use
it will simply be rooted again.)

So always be on the lookout for these extra colour treats
which Nature sends from time to time. Something a little
different keeps one's inspiration flowing.

Colour-Sense Can Be Learned

The more subtlety you can get into the colour scheme of a
flower arrangement, the better. Even a tiny graduation of
colouring in a couple of leaves can make that important
difference between an ordinarily competent flower design
and a real work of art. Colour-sense is something which
can be learned—by observation.

It's surprising how many people are blind to just one
colour, which they do not see true. They can still enjoy
flower arranging, however, by avoiding their blind spot
colour.

If you find colour a real problem in your flower arranging; begin arranging flowers of one colour only, with their
own foliage or with contrasting leaves. I used to think it
safe to blend not more than three different colours in one
arrangement, with "neutral" unobtrusive background
leaves, and I would advise beginners to adopt this rule. It
soon becomes easier to fit in additional hues while still
maintaining a pleasing and satisfying harmony.

Taking part in shows and exhibitions is a great help
towards a good colour-sense, because one always goes to
a little extra trouble to seek out a leaf or flower of
exactly the right colour and tone. And, seeing what other
people are doing with their material is always instruct-
ive.

But try not to copy—it shouldn't be necessary, anyway,

for there are so many gradations and delicacies of colour in everything that grows.

A Tonic to the Spirit

Colour can be a tonic to the spirit. Everyone knows how exhilarating is the first arrangement of golden daffodils. When you're having a blue day mix yourself a good, strong, vibrant flower arrangement for the house. See how it helps.

For such an arrangement, take bold chances with the colours. Crash together pinks, reds, scarlets of any shade and tint. Or bring together orange, coral, yellow and gold in another dramatic splash. When the sun is shining and the house is very bright, on the other hand, use colour more sparingly. But never get into a rut.

Don't be afraid to ring the changes. Have a go at an arrangement of bright blue flowers with olive green and tan foliage in a light-coloured wooden container, just for the fun of it. Or try the effect of tan-coloured and grey-green leaves with flowers of terra-cotta colour in a matt black container. Play around with soft pink blooms against pale yellow foliage in well-polished silver.

How Artists Do It

The advanced flower arranger often prefers to gently underplay colour rather than overstress it, and will offset any bright colour with one which is quieter. As mastery of the art is achieved an appreciation of pastel and off-beat colourings is invariably born.

Study pictures, any kind of pictures. As a flower arranger you make your pictures with flowers not oil paints, but you can learn a great deal about colour by looking at paintings. See how some artists use little touches of many colours to make up a satisfying whole, while others get their effects by using only one or two *colours* but many *tones*. Note, too, how some landscape paintings which seem to be all the green of countryside and the blue of sky are actually full of other colours, subtly worked in so that the eye is deceived yet delighted.

The eye is, indeed, constantly tricked and pleased by colour. Artists know that blues tend to recede from the eye (see how they use blues near the horizon in a landscape, to give the effect of distance), while reds come forward. A touch of red makes greens come alive, and warm colours are set off against cold ones. The warm colours are the reds, browns, oranges, and sunny yellows; cold colours are the greens and blues. To express it another way, any colour which is near to red is warm, any which is tending towards blue is cold.

Containers and Colours

Containers should always be chosen with careful thought as to their suitability of colour and texture, as well as shape. On starting an arrangement, take out a couple of different containers and hold them against your bunch of flowers. Is, say, a white urn going to be better than a copper bowl? When you see containers and material together it is not too hard to make the right choice. Not until you are sure that the flowers and the container are made for each other should you get down to arranging.

Why Texture Is Important

Everyone understands that various fabrics have distinctive textures, and we make use of this in furnishing and decoration. In just the same way, we make use of the contrasting textures of flowers and leaves. All kinds of finesse in design is possible when you place satin-smooth petals against the contrast of rough-textured leaves, feathery flowers against smooth foliage, or a heavily

112

ribbed leaf against a plain one. The qualities of each are intensified and the finished arrangement has added interest and that wonderful extra touch of magic and mystery.

Containers have differing textures, too, and this should be taken into account just like colour and shape. In show and exhibition work, the nice balance and interplay of textures is important, particularly with regard to drapes and bases for interpretive classes.

The various do's and dont's cannot always be rigidly applied—making a flower arrangement is not like following a knitting pattern. Don't hesitate to experiment; you will have your favourite tints, shades and textures, but it's good to get away from them every now and then. This is the way to develop a real all-round understanding of colour which will greatly add to your command of flower arranging—and to your decorating and dress sense, too.

CHAPTER 8

Clubs and Flower Shows

To derive the fullest delight from arranging flowers I
would certainly advise everyone to join a club. There are
scores of these, all over the country, and in them one
meets women (and men) who are keen to explore and
develop the art in all its forms.

If your club is anything like mine, you'll meet lots of
pleasant people, as well as finding that you learn very much
more painlessly than if you struggle on alone.

Most clubs meet monthly, and programmes generally
consist of demonstrations, talks, practice evenings, films
and so on. Shows are held by clubs individually and in
collaboration with one another. Often the ordinary
monthly meeting includes an exhibition, or competitive
classes of members' arrangements.

Many clubs, too, run a sales stall at their meetings, at
which you can buy pinholders, chicken wire, flowers,
plants and dried material, and other useful items at a little
below shop prices.

If your club has a monthly competition, or a small competitive exhibition at each meeting, don't hesitate to take
part. These little shows are fun, they test your ingenuity,
provide you with ideas, prevent you getting into a rut, and
prepare you for even bigger and better shows and competitions. Usually, club shows are divided into sections
for "Novices," "Intermediate," and "Advanced" members
—so you are always certain of a fair chance right from your

earliest days and you move from one section to the next when you gain the required number of points.

Try for a Prize

When you have belonged to a flower club for a time and have gained confidence by taking part in the monthly competitions, try out your skill at a bigger show. In time you can progress to the big national shows, such as those run by the National Association of Flower Arrangement Societies, the Royal National Rose Society, and others. You can join the various specialist societies, such as the National Rose Society, for a few shillings a year, and they are excellent value not only for the chance of exhibiting your favourite flowers but also because of their various facilities and publications.

Study the Schedule

Before sending in your entry for a show, study the schedule (or programme of classes) carefully and select the class or classes which you feel able to tackle most confidently, and for which you will have containers and material available on the day of the show. Don't attempt too many classes.

When you do your arrangements it is essential to abide *exactly* by what the schedule says—the judge certainly will! For example, if the class is "An Arrangement of Leaves and Berries" you are allowed to use *only* leaves and berries, not flowers. A wise old show motto is "When in doubt, leave out."

Unfortunately, some schedules (especially at very small shows, church fêtes, and similar functions) are badly and ambiguously worded, and both exhibitors and judges are left wondering exactly what the committee had in mind. If in doubt, ask the show secretary to get a ruling.

As a judge, I know that many otherwise praiseworthy

entries have to be disqualified at almost every show because they are "not according to schedule." No judge likes having to disqualify, but it is the only way to be fair to those exhibitors who have taken the trouble to study the schedule and abide by it.

With or Without Accessories

The first thing about which you must be certain is whether the class you are entering is for an arrangement, or what used to be called a composition but is now referred to as "An arrangement with one or more accessories." If you are asked, in a Show schedule, to make "A design" this means you can include one or more accessories *if you wish*.

"An arrangement" is defined as being of natural plant material in any container, with or without a base. More than one container may be used, but the plant material must appear to be in a single grouping, and accessories should not be used.

An accessory is an ornament, plate, figurine, candle, or similar piece of non-plant material. Stones, shells, and similar objects are usually considered to be accessories unless otherwise stated in the schedule.

Incidentally, if you belong to a recognised flower arrangement club or society you can get a copy of the 1967 booklet, "Schedule Definitions," published by the National Association of Flower Arrangement Societies, which is an invaluable guide for schedule compilers, exhibitors, and adjudicators.

Aids to Show Work

If you do much show work, a plastic sponge-bag with a zip or press-stud top is handy for carrying all your bits and pieces, such as flower scissors, rubber bands, modelling clay, stub wires, spare pinholders, pins, a tape measure, a roll of sticky tape, and a duster or absorbent cloth for mopping up water. Pop in your purse, hanky and make-up and you won't need to take a handbag.

A small sheet of transparent plastic placed under your container will keep the table (or your drape) clean and dry while you work.

Preparation Pays

For your first show, aim at doing a simple, neat, well-designed entry in just one class. Get to the show tent or hall in good time, and quietly set to work. Don't rush. Don't be discouraged if the exhibitor next to you is doing an absolutely superb piece of work—one always tends to think one's own work is inferior, especially early in the day. When you return later, the arrangement always looks better than you thought.

One of the secrets of successful show work is careful preparation on the day before the show. Choose the flowers and container and any accessories unhurriedly; prepare the flowers and leaves in the manner described in an earlier chapter. If you intend to do more than one arrangement, keep the materials for each in separate buckets or jugs.

Sort out your containers, and secure wire netting or pinholders firmly inside the chosen ones. Put with them a small watering can with a long spout. *Check up* to see that you have everything you need.

Working at Home

I have found that if a show is not too far from home it is best to do the arrangement at home, rather than in the show tent. (That is, unless the schedule and rules of the show specify that all work must be done on the spot.) If you are at all nervous or highly-strung you will probably work best at home. At most shows you will have to put up your exhibit early in the morning (usually before 11 a.m.), so an added advantage of doing the work at home is that you can do it the previous evening and avoid the risk of an early-morning scramble.

In such a case, the flowers and leaves need to be picked or bought the morning before the show, any buds tied, a long drink given throughout the afternoon, and the arrangement produced in the evening. The completed design should have its water level checked and should finally be placed in the coolest and darkest spot you can find. In hot weather, sprinkle the flowers with water.

Enthusiastic beginners have been known to arrive at a show bearing two arrangements for one class, having done the two at home and then found it impossible to decide which to enter. They often ask whether they can submit both, but this is rarely allowed. Some shows even limit entries in each class to one person per family, so as to be scrupulously fair to all competitors.

A Popular Class

To judge from many hundreds of letters I've received, one of the most popular show classes ever devised is "An Arrangement for a Hot Day." But though it is such a favourite with organisers and committees, many exhibitors ask "What does it mean?"

The title simply means an arrangement of flowers in cool, refreshing colours, such as white, blue and green. Any colours and textures, in fact, which make you feel cool. The hot colours (orange, red, deep pink, tan, etc.) are unsuitable.

The container for this class is an important consideration. Remember that silver looks cooler than brass or copper. A mirror, as a base under the container, reflects light and gives an impression of coolness and tranquillity. Water always looks cool, so you could use a long shallow container with the arrangement at one end, leaving an expanse of clear water.

Where Ideas Come From

How does one get ideas for show exhibits? People new to the hobby always ask this question. After talking to exhibitors at very many shows I have collected a variety of ways of producing ideas. One competitor said she read her schedule last thing one evening about a fortnight before a show—and invariably woke up next morning with one or two good designs in mind!

Another exhibitor assured me she had her brightest ideas in the bath, and yet another while ironing. I have a friend who always rides her bicycle into the country on the day before a show to gather leaves, wild flowers, fungi, and other wild material, which she finds a constant source of inspiration.

A more practical method than any of the above is to walk around the garden or go along to the florist's shop a week before the show. You then get a good idea what flowers will be available when you want them, and seeing flowers like this will probably suggest just the right idea.

When you have the germ of an arrangement in your mind, don't be tempted to over-elaborate it and make it too clever. The most successful flower showpieces have a clear-cut idea portrayed with simplicity. Don't try to cram too much into an arrangement—you can spoil the whole thing by not knowing when to stop.

Think Systematically

A proved way of summoning ideas to mind is to write down every thought which comes into your head about the class you have chosen to enter. For example, the class might be entitled "Housewife's Choice—An arrangement of any natural material, suitable for a sideboard." Think systematically around this theme.

"Any natural material"—This can include fruit, leaves, flowers, driftwood, or anything else which is growing or has grown. Plenty of scope here.

"Housewife's Choice"—Perhaps this suggests a busy woman with many jobs on her hands, so a rather simple design might be more suitable than an intricate one, with common garden flowers preferable to more exotic blooms from the florist.

"Suitable for a sideboard"—This certainly calls to mind colourful, luscious fruit, and rules out fungi, poisonous berries, and similar material.

Now you have something to work on. Gather the material together, pick out one or two containers, and "play around" with them for a while. Soon a design will begin to form—the best kind of design, for it will be dictated by the material and container themselves. This is always better than trying to force the material and make it fit some vague notion in your mind's eye.

Ideas by Accident

Ideas come rolling in to me from all kinds of places. The other day, for instance, one of my dogs brought me a stick to throw for him, just when I was trying to think how to do a design for a show class called "An Age of Man." The stick was twisted and weather-worn, and it at once was reminiscent of old age. With suitable accessories and flowers, the twig was used in my arrangement to put over the feeling of age.

In general, however, I find that my own best inspiration comes from seeing and handling flowers, or from finding just the right colourings in a few well-shaped leaves. With practice and experience it is possible to turn out a presentable and attractive arrangement every time, but occasionally a really great idea presents itself, the right flowers bloom to perfection on the right day, and the design almost literally arranges itself.

Flowers Aren't Funny

Flower arranging is fun—but it never pays to try to be *funny* with flowers; they are not suited to it. I recall a "Mood" class in which an exhibitor had thrown a few blue flowers into a niche with a brown drape and a vase and the title "Fed Up." Well, it wasn't a flower arrangement.

The craziest show I ever entered had 20 classes. One was entitled "Fun with flowers—An arrangement to make you laugh." The winner had done her design in an old boot with a bit cut away to show a corn flower in place of a corn plaster.

Is It the Right Size?

Show schedules usually state the amount of space allowed for exhibits in each class—for example, "To be staged in a niche 36 inches wide." Beginners are sometimes puzzled by such directions, and wonder why they loose points when their arrangement is either too large or too small.

A niche is reserved for each arrangement, the niches being made from neutral coloured pieces of thick card or corrugated paper. Niches are put up by the show committee and will be in position when you arrive. Niches, or some similar background setting for the exhibits, are known as the backing.

When doing an exhibit at home, before a show, I pin a tape measure to the table to show me the exact size of the niche. If I do an arrangement at the show itself, I work in the niche.

Never allow your flowers or leaves to touch the sides of the niche, nor, on the other hand, make the design so small that it looks lost in the centre of the space allowed. Always think of your arrangement as a picture; the space you leave round is the frame.

The arrangement should always be in good proportion to the size of the niche. An arrangement which is too small can be made to look larger if raised on a base.

A symmetrical design looks well when the container is placed in the centre of the niche; it often looks even better just off-centre. With other designs, try them in various positions in the niche to see where they have the best effect.

Using a Drape

A drape is a piece, or pieces, of fabric chosen with care to complement or make a background for the flowers, leaves, etc., and the container. Nowadays one is allowed to use a drape in every class unless the schedule specifically forbids it.

A drape is easily secured to the niche or other backing with a straight pin, a couple of paper clips, or merely by draping (hence the name) over the top of the backing. I once bought a tall, old-fashioned wooden hat stand from a millinery shop which was closing down, and this has proved invaluable for holding up a drape behind an exhibit. The little round cushion at the top, where the hat used to go, is ready-made for pinning the drape in position. Friends with handymen husbands have had similar supports made from pieces of dowelling fixed to a firm base.

About a yard and a half of material is required to make

a useful drape. For small arrangements you may get away with a yard, but unless the material is rather wide this can prove inadequate. Drapes and swirling bases may be made from a variety of fabrics—velvet, silk, cotton, rayon, fine woven straw, tulle, organza, etc. Drapes may also be of card, coloured felt, or wood-grained paper. The soft furnishings and dress fabrics departments of the big stores—at sale times!—are the best and cheapest places for buying drapes. Always buy one good-quality piece of material rather than two cheap ones. The better, heavier materials drape into rich folds, they last longer, and they have an altogether more satisfying appearance.

Points may be lost if your drape or base is creased and crumpled, so carry it to the show in a rolled up newspaper or wrapped around a cylinder of cardboard (most fabric departments will be only too pleased to make you a present of these cylinders if you ask).

Try to build up a collection of drapes in different fabrics and different colours. You can't have too many; you never know when any one of them will be just right for a given arrangement.

Be Sparing with Accessories

An accessory is something extra—a figurine or other ornament, perhaps — used with the flowers and other plant material to enhance the design or to give it special point.

Accessories can be delightful but they can also be a danger, for so many people have a weakness for adding lots of bits and pieces, the result being a design which is messy and cluttered. It is like wearing too much jewellery on a flowered dress.

The point to bear in mind is that the accessories should always be secondary to the flowers. A drape, one figurine and a title card will in most cases be all that is needed. The larger the niche, the larger the arrangement, and the larger the accessories can be.

Take care when using driftwood, nuts, or fruit in an exhibit. If any of these is placed separately from the main design the whole thing becomes an arrangement with accessories.

The Driftwood Vogue

There's a vogue for driftwood in flower arranging nowadays. As explained earlier, any piece of wood which has weathered naturally is called driftwood . . . it's not necessary to have found it on the seashore! I once had a letter from an old lady in Scotland who asked where she could buy driftwood; the only thing she could find was half a tree blown down the river in a gale! I wrote to her, and heard later that she won first prize in her class at a show, using curved branches of burned gorse, blackened in a fire on the moorland near her home. With the charred branches she used scarlet geranium flowers and pieces of white clematis in seed.

Grey and brown driftwood always associates well with dried or preserved materials as well as with wild flowers, berries, leaves, fungi, etc., and with stones, wooden figurines, and many garden flowers. Choose a piece of wood with a good shape and it will set your imagination going and be a fruitful source of ideas. It may be bleached, but being natural plant material it should not be painted, except possibly at Christmas time.

Before starting an arrangement turn your hunk of driftwood around in your hands; look at it from every angle.

124

If it has a natural curve, let your flowers, leaves, seedheads and so on follow this shape. You will sometimes find a piece which resembles a bird, animal, or human figure, so play up to this and accentuate it—build your arrangement round it.

Title Cards

Show schedules often require that each exhibit be given a title, or else a card stating the theme and perhaps naming the varieties of flowers used. Exhibitors sometimes lose points by writing on scrappy bits of paper or grubby card. Again, cards are frequently out of scale with the arrangement (too large or too small), or so badly placed that they make too much of themselves and spoil the appearance of the whole exhibit.

Why should such a small detail be so important, you may ask. Surely if the flower arrangement is a good one, the judge will overlook something so small and insignificant as the title card. And so she may at a small show of the kind put on at a village fête, but at a show organised by a flower arrangement club or one of the specialist horticultural societies you are up against keen competition, with judges trained to observe the smallest details. In fact, when two exhibits are equally good it is the most minute considerations which finally decide the award.

I always feel that it is important to pay attention to details, on the principle that if a thing is worth doing it is worth doing well. Take care of the small points, and the standard of your work will automatically be raised.

The title card should be planned as part of the exhibit, not added as an afterthought. It should be neatly and clearly lettered or typewritten. Thin card looks better than paper. The colour of the card must be taken into account; it should tie in with the colour of the flowers, leaves, or container, or with the colour of the backing.

I save Christmas cards and birthday cards and cut them up for title cards. Quite frequently, a bit of the printed design on a greetings card—a pink rosebud, say—will prove exactly right to match an arrangement. I find, too, that a wavy edge to a card is better than a straight one, so I always cut mine to gently curving shapes.

Title cards look best if tilted slightly towards the eye. A favourite prop of mine is a rose pink, velvet-covered Victorian pin-cushion shaped like a heart (bought for sixpence at a jumble sale). This makes a charming background for a title card on many occasions.

Remember that if you use a card (unless it is specifically demanded in the schedule) it counts as an accessory, because it is a secondary placement.

Nerves at Showtime

Most women suffer a temporary affliction known as show nerves when they first take part in a flower arrangement show. It's stage fright, and it passes off quite quickly, as any old hand will tell you. An aspirin and a hot drink the night before the show, last thing, will help you to sleep well. At the show, suck barley sugar while you work, and have a break for a hot drink from a vacuum flask.

A final word about competitive flower arranging—don't take it too seriously or take failure personally. If you don't win a prize, be nice to the more successful exhibitors. Never argue with the judge; hers is a difficult task, not lightly undertaken. And remember there's always another show.

Organising a Show

If you begin to take an active part in the life of your flower club or society you will probably find yourself taking part in organising a show.

I happen to prefer shows in marquees rather than in halls during the summer. The diffused light under canvas is kind to flowers and foliage, and there is none of the distraction of strong sunlight pouring through windows. True, the canvas may flap in windy weather and knock down arrangements or backing—but not if a sensible space has been left between the tables and the tent wall. Backing won't blow down if it is pinned to the table or fastened to wooden battens driven into the ground behind the table.

When you're helping to put up a show in a marquee borrow a spirit level to make sure the tables are level. Because of uneven ground and wobbly tables I have found it wise to use only firm, heavy containers when showing under canvas. Tall, slim containers or pieces of delicate china are best kept for an indoor occasion.

At two-day or three-day shows, or in hot weather, proper arrangements must be made to replace faded blooms and to top up the water in all containers. After all, it should be a point of honour to present the public with a sight worth seeing whether they come in immediately after the opening on the first day or five minutes before closing time on the last.

The British climate being what it is, most shows are sensibly held indoors. Good facilities for the exhibitors to do their arrangements are a must. I hold painful memories of shows where exhibitors were not allowed to work in the hall itself, but only in a cramped backstage area. A word with the hall caretaker may be necessary to ensure that the hall heating is suitably regulated; the hall

127

must not be so warm that the lasting properties of the flowers are endangered. At one autumn show put on by my flower club an over-keen caretaker got the place so hot that the white plastic table coverings began to bubble.

Sunshine portends well for a show (if only because the public are more likely to turn out in fine weather), but flowers open quickly in the warmer weather, particularly those belonging to the exhibitor who finds herself with a position in full sunshine. A single sheet of newspaper makes a very good sunshade if gently placed over a completed arrangement until it is time for judging to start. If the arrangement is not too big, place it in the shade under the table until judging time.

Sprinkling flowers and leaves with a hand dipped in cool water decidedly helps in hot, dry weather—but be careful not to mark your drape. Some people use light, fine spray atomisers to provide humidity for their flowers in an arrangement. Plastic spray bottles which do the same job can be bought quite cheaply from the chain stores.

CHAPTER 9

For Special Occasions

Sooner or later there comes a grand occasion, a special celebration, when a flower arrangement just a little different from the usual run of things is required. It may be a christening, a wedding, a birthday, or a Christmas party. Flowers will play their special role in conveying good wishes, imparting an air of festivity, giving a welcome, or creating a feeling of gaiety.

All parties, for any age group, need a flower centre-piece which makes a talking point. This focal point of the room need not be the table, which will already be bright and colourful with good food and drink. Elsewhere in the room, place a flower arrangement which is both striking and original.

For the Birthday Tea

If the party is for youngsters, it's a good thing to keep traditional-style flower arrangements to a minimum. If you do have them, place them on something solid, and well out of reach. Anything pretty or fine in design will be lost on children; the younger the children, the more vividly coloured the decorations need to be. Red, orange, and yellow will make more of an impression than pastels.

For very young tots, don't bother with real flowers at all. They will be much more impressed with bigger-than-life-size "flowers" cut out of stiff card or coloured tissue paper. Coloured card can be bought quite inexpensively, and it is not difficult to cut out the simple shapes of bluebells, daisies, snowdrops and daffodils. Then using drawing pins or sticky tape to fasten flowers and leaves to stems made from lengths of green plant stakes. Arrange them in a sturdy pottery vase with real leaves for the best effect.

Both boys and girls like a silver tree at a party. Make one by filling a large well-scrubbed plant pot with Poly-filla and inserting a shapely, twiggy branch, minus its foliage. Paint tree and pot silver, gold or white.

When the paint is dry the tree can be decorated with sweets in shiny papers, tied on with cotton, and with real or marzipan fruit. Stand the tree where it catches the light, or place it opposite the door of the party room, where it can be seen at once. Smaller trees, similarly decorated, can be made to stand on the tea table. Being twiggy they don't obscure the view, and being tall they take up very little actual table space. Instead of a table-cloth, use coloured crêpe paper or silver kitchen foil.

For Older Children

Small boys aren't very interested in flowers as a rule, but I once made an enormously successful table centre at a party for ten-year-old boys. In a shallow pottery cooking dish with a pinholder at one end I arranged reeds and bright yellow iris; the pinholder was covered with stones. In the remaining area of the dish two live goldfish swam about.

As small girls grow up they notice flowers more, especially if encouraged to arrange them. They like pretty flowers, and this often means small ones. At one party, for 12-13 year-old girls, I made an individual Victorian posy for each place setting, to match a larger one in the centre of the table. Each nosegay had the stems cut rather short, so that they sat comfortably in a little water dish hidden by a napkin ring. Ribbons connected the various posies to the centrepiece.

Teen-age Parties

Informality is the keynote of the teen-age party. Maybe there's a barbecue, or else food is served straight from the kitchen or in the garden from an informal buffet table. Kitchens can be made to look very gay with bowls of fruit, checked gingham cloths, strings of onions, flickering candles in empty beer and wine bottles, and perhaps an arrangement of garden flowers and vegetables in a basket.

One of the best designs of this kind I have ever seen was a low arrangement of white daisies, red geraniums, and yellow snapdragons, which exactly picked up the colours in salads of ripe tomatoes, sliced hard-boiled eggs, and spring onions.

Out of doors, hang lamps and lanterns decorated with leaves, fruits, and flowers. A porcel of damp Stemfix in foil is tied to each lamp to take the stems. Candles or electric torches inside the lanterns provide the light if wiring from the house is too difficult.

A large trug basket of potted geraniums is wonderfully effective on an outdoor serving table. If you're lucky enough to have a garden pool or fountain, turn it into a giant flower arrangement by floating pale yellow or white flower-heads on the water.

Crystallised Flowers

Weddings, birthdays, christenings, and Christmas parties have natural focal points in the traditional iced cake. You can make unusual and extremely beautiful cake decorations by crystallising fresh flowers. Any flower which is sweet-scented is edible. If carefully stored, crystallised flowers will keep for many years; I know of some which have been kept successfully for ten years.

Delicate pink and blue cornflowers look lovely when crystallised, as do primroses, delphinium "pips," pansies, forget-me-nots, daisies and sprigs of heather. For the process you need cake colouring in the same colours as the flowers, caster sugar, granulated sugar, rosewater and gum arabic. Mix together two parts of caster sugar to one part of granulated, on a saucer, and carefully add drops of the appropriate colouring. Crush with a spoon and put through a sieve to remove lumps. Next mix three to four teaspoonfuls of rosewater to one teaspoonful of powdered gum arabic.

With a fine camel hair brush, paint the front and back of each flower with the rosewater and gum arabic solution, carefully supporting the flower on your third finger as you work. Don't be too heavy-handed with the solution. Finally, sprinkle both sides of the flower with the sugar mixture. Then all you have to do is leave the flowers to dry out on a wire cake cooler for about a week, afterwards storing them in cardboard boxes or tins with air holes in the lids, in a very dry cupboard.

A Golden Wedding . . .

A golden wedding celebration naturally suggests making the fullest use of golden flowers and golden leaves, arranged in gilded or white containers. There are many glorious flowers of golden hue, and it is a good idea to plant extra annuals of yellow and gold in a year when a golden wedding is to be celebrated in the family. This is the kind of occasion which demands big, sumptuously joyful flower arrangements, so you can't have too many flowers.

There are dozens of different golden leaves, from such

striking plants as eleagnus, golden holly, golden privet, variegated periwinkle, variegated ivy (several varieties throw gold-splashed leaves) and variegated New Zealand flax.

... and a Silver Wedding

Silver weddings can be more difficult, and the tendency is to end up with an arrangement of pastel-coloured flowers which can look very ordinary. There are, however, many grey leaves which look enchanting when arranged with white flowers, and some of these are as near silver as makes no difference.

Shrubby convolvulus (*Convolvulus Cneorum*) is a special pet of mine for dining table decorations, and at certain times of year it has a really silvery sheen to its leaf. Pussy willow, too, looks silvery, and many clematis seedheads have the soft glow of old silver. When the blue flowers of Cupid's Dart (*Catananche Caerulea*) have fallen they leave behind a little rustling silver shuttlecock which dries and keeps its colour admirably and is well-suited to small arrangements. The bud is silver, too.

Other silver and grey foliage plants include garden ragwort and plume poppy (used back to front, to show the reverse of the leaves), carnation, pink, southernwood, grevillea, lavender, lamb's ear, catmint, rosemary and some varieties of begonia rex.

Pressed filigree ferns and preserved sweet chestnut leaves can be painted silver and arranged with sprays of silvered honesty. Add shimmering artificial flowers made up from pink nylon organza, and you have an original and eye-catching arrangement. The artificial flowers are made quite quickly. Cut out petal shapes from the fabric and, with a long length of fine fuse wire or florist's wire, attach one petal at a time to a thicker strand of wire, until there are sufficient petals to suggest a full or budded rose.

Flowers for a Dance

For a private dance, one large pedestal arrangement as a welcome in the hall, foyer, or entrance, a second in the ballroom, and a third, smaller, design in the ladies' room are possibly all the flowers you will require. In the ballroom, flower arrangements should stand high so that they can be seen. Deep containers are a must, for the warmth of the hall will quickly evaporate the water, especially on a summer evening.

If there is to be a principal lady or guest of honour it is a happy thought to work out the flower colour schemes to complement her dress, if the colour of this is known beforehand. I once arranged the flowers for a dance at which a famous model and television commère, was to present the prizes. We took our keynote from her own pink and white colouring, and we learned also that she was to wear a silver-pink dress. So all the flowers were of delicate pastel pinks and white, and when she arrived we presented her with a matching posy.

Arrangements for the Table

Modern dining tables are not usually large. The days of big families and long tables have gone, and flower decorations for them have shrunk, too. Plenty of room must be allowed for place settings and serving dishes, and it is better to have the flower arrangement a little too small rather than too large.

A container with a short stem, such as a low candlestick (with a candle-cup holder for the flowers) is ideal for a dining table centre. Everyone can see the flowers, but very little table space is taken up. For all tables, of course, you must have a design which does not obscure the view. If only two or three people are using the table, a rather different layout can be made, with the flowers arranged at one end rather than in the centre. In this position quite a tall design is possible, perhaps balanced by a bowl of fruit at the other end of the table.

Though a modern table demands a rather slick-looking flower arrangement, a table which is antique or just old-fashioned dark polished wood will happily take almost any style of arrangement, depending on the other table appointments. My own antique dining table can one day appear rather grand with silver candelabra, fine china, and crisply starched napkins, and the following day be completely different, with sturdy modern pottery, woven straw mats in gay colours, and riotously bright flowers and leaves arranged to catch this mood.

When arranging flowers for a dining table, take care that their colours (and that of the container) go with the decor of the room. Your material must always be in first-class condition (no drooping flowers here) because it will be seen at close range.

Flowers for a Wedding

If you are asked to do the flowers for a wedding (I don't mean the bouquets and buttonholes) take the earliest opportunity of looking round the church, and ask the vicar to enter your name on the church's flower rota for the day of the ceremony. This is advisable to avoid clashing with the church's own regular flower arrangers. In the church, decide where you will put your arrangements, how many flowers will be required for each container, and how tall your designs will need to be so that they can be seen even when the congregation is standing. Take account of whether the flowers will be seen against dark or light backgrounds, so that you can use appropriately contrasting tones.

Find out whether the vicar allows flowers on the altar, or whether he has any views about the placing of the arrangements generally. When I did the flowers for my sister's wedding, I remember, I used a large pedestal design against the pulpit, little dreaming that on such an occasion the vicar would go into the pulpit to preach. But he did, and he had the greatest difficulty squeezing past the arrangement and avoiding sending it cascading in a broken wet mess to the floor.

What Colours To Use?

Flower colours for a church wedding depend to some extent upon the time of the year and whether your budget runs to out-of-season blooms. As a principle, try to use flowers in colours which blend with the bride's or bridesmaids' dresses. For a white wedding, white flowers always look stunning. If the bride does not like all-white flowers in the church, use white ones plus some in the same colouring as the bridesmaids' gowns. Lilies are particularly suited to such an occasion, and even if you cannot use them elsewhere try to have a few on the altar.

If you are going to use flowers from the florist, do order them well in advance. A good florist will always try to get exactly the varieties and colours you need, and will be helped by snippets of dress material which you may wish to match. Have the flowers delivered in good time the day before the wedding so that they can have their pre-arrangement deep drink.

Pedestal Arrangements

A pedestal arrangement is indispensable to any occasion which requires a tall, elegant, or dominant design and

which needs important flowers. All pedestal arrangements require flowers and leaves in abundance—long
branches, big leaves and flowers full of character, rather
than dozens of small-sized blooms and leaves. The
arrangement must be conceived on the grand scale.

What about the pedestal itself? In essence, this is merely
a tall stand of wood or metal with a bowl or trough at the
top. Specially made ones, with a trough incorporated,
can be bought, or a blacksmith will make one to your own
design. A handyman could convert one of those tall
stands made to hold birdcages, or could adapt an old
standard lamp. Junk shops and auction sale rooms sometimes have tall wooden plinths (often made like classical
columns) which used to hold marble busts, and the same
sources may yield quite cheaply, a Victorian floor-standing
oil lamp in wrought iron or brass. For a low pedestal
arrangement, a wine table is ideal. What really counts
most is that the pedestal should be well-balanced
and not easily tipped over. Weight at the base is an
advantage.

Before commencing a pedestal arrangement it is absolutely vital to see that the thing is standing firmly and that
the bowl or trough is really secure. Remember that it
has to carry a lot of weight, most of which will be towards the front. Inside the container I always use a large
pinholder as well as chicken wire, to grip those important
back stems. As you work, step back frequently to view the
effect from the other end of the hall, down the aisle, or
across the room.

A strong, firm outline shape is essential. More often
than not, pedestal flowers are arranged to triangular or
fan-shaped silhouettes, but there is no reason why you
should not have a large Hogarth curve. When two
pedestals are to stand either side of a doorway or stage

137

they can well be arranged as assymetrical triangles or as opposite crescents.

Some flowers and leaves should be brought below the level of the container (which may or may not be hidden), and it is a good idea to bring some out at the back also. This gives the arrangement depth, helps to balance the weight at the front, and looks well when the arrangement is seen from the side.

Use fruit, sprays of berries, seedheads, and even driftwood in pedestal designs. At Christmas or party time, painted and glittered material is effective. Any plant material with a built-in downwards growth is ideal for placing low down in a pedestal arrangement—things like trails of hops, vines, old man's beard, clematis, Virginia creeper, and rambler or climbing roses.

People often ask how tall a pedestal arrangement should be. The only guide is to study the height of the room and then make your arrangement of an appropriate size. A room or hall with a high ceiling will take a very tall arrangement; a long, low room necessitates something smaller. It's a matter of relying on your eye.

Giving a Present

On many occasions a gift of flowers is more appropriate than an expensive present. Happily, even a few homely garden flowers can be given the million-dollar look when cleverly arranged. To congratulate a new mother after the birth of a baby, take her an arrangement of pink and white flowers if it's a girl, blue and white for a boy. A knot of ribbons among the flowers gives the expensive look. Arrange flowers and foliage in moist Stemfix.

Many florists sell small wicker baskets with lids, and these make attractive containers for the smaller flowers. Or you can buy pint-sized canework cots and prams, complete with tin linings to hold the water for flowers; these can be made up into the prettiest things imaginable if you place the flowers inside so that they resemble the baby in its cot. From small white flowerheads (such as snowy arabis) make the shape of the pillow and the turn-down of the sheet, and use forget-me-nots or pink stocks for the coverlet. Suggest the head of the baby with a pink rosebud on the white pillow, and add a bow of ribbon and a card to complete the gift.

A Victorian posy of small, sweet-scented, pastel-coloured flowers can be made by threading the stems of the flowers, in rings of different colours, through the centre holes of a plastic doily. The edge of the doily is left to form a frill. The posy always starts off with a rosebud, and is finished off with a ribbon bow and trails at the back. If you put the doily on the top of a water-filled jam jar before commencing the arrangement you will find this keeps the stems in position while you work. Bind the stems with a rubber band or florist's wire, and finish off with a wrapping of silver foil.

Once won over to the notion of giving a flower arrangement instead of just a bunch of flowers as a present, many fresh ways come to mind. When visiting a new mother and her baby, for example, do the arrangement in a container which is in itself a present for the baby—a christening mug or a silver spoon, for instance.

A Miniature Garden

For a sick person or a mother-to-be, make a miniature garden. Take a large plate or a meat dish, and fill with peat or moist earth. Plant such things as a tiny seedling tree, bits of rockery plants just coming into flower, a small fern, or any little subjects which are almost in flower. Pop in a few well-shaped stones or pebbles to resemble rocks, and sink into the earth one or two empty fish paste jars which will hold water for a few little cut flowers. Cover the earth and the jars with moss.

A little imagination and ingenuity will enable you to work many variations on this garden-in-a-plate idea for all sorts of occasions. These gardens will last for some weeks if kept in a good light and watered only when the soil feels dry to the touch.

To Cheer the Sick

Flowers always make a delightful gift for anyone who is ill, at home or in hospital, and how much more attractive they are when made into an arrangement. A simple, compact design and a container which can be easily transported are needed, and the use of Stemfix or Oasis means that you have no water problem. (But don't forget the deep drink first.) Fruit, especially black or green grapes, and eggs can be worked into the arrangement instead of being taken in a paper bag.

When taking flowers to the sick, avoid the very strongly-scented, which may seem heady and cloying to an invalid. I prefer to use slightly-perfumed flowers, adding leaves which give off a fragrance when pinched. Herbs such as balm or marjoram (and of course lavender and mint) are a refreshing addition to the design.

Don't use lilies (still associated with funerals in people's minds), or red and white flowers together, for many nurses have a superstition about these two colours together.

Happy Christmas

Time spent during the summer and autumn in pressing and preserving leaves and seedheads brings its reward at Christmas, when they can be painted gold, white, and silver to make enchanting decorations. Paint colourless nail varnish round the edges of some leaves and along some branches, and while it is wet sprinkle it with sparkling "frost," bought from the chain stores in packets. Be careful not to get this near food, as it is usually made from powdered glass.

Artificial snow, which is strong enough to hold leaves and other preserved materials in a container, can be made by mixing soap powder to a very stiff consistency with a little water. The mixture goes quite hard, but is afterwards easily washed out with hot water. Another quick-setting holder for stems is Polyfilla (Alabastine is similar). Bits of hollowed-out log, empty dog meat tins, little foil dishes which have held frozen food, are all expendable containers which can be used for Christmas arrangements and afterwards thrown away.

Generally speaking, glittered material does not blend comfortably with fresh flowers and foliage, so the two should be kept apart.

The traditional evergreens last without water throughout the Christmas festivities, and there are many ways of using them. One of my favourites is a low basket or garden trug filled with holly, ivy, etc., with the rich dark greens setting off the merry colours of shining Christmas tree baubles, apples and oranges.

Glossy evergreens look specially Christmassy if lightly brushed with shoe whitener, bought in a tube. White, gold, and silver paints come in spray cans nowadays, and these are handy though not very economical.

Fruit, with all its fresh, mouth-watering colour, can take the place of flowers in all kinds of designs made with evergreens and preserved leaves. Baskets, silver dishes, and any containers made of glowing brass or copper are perfect settings for fruit arrangements. If the container is large, fill it first with chicken wire and pile up the fruit on top.

Grapes, both green and black, give distinction to a fruit arrangement, and indeed I find them so decorative that I sometimes make a design purely from grapes. As with all fruit arrangements for the home, one just doesn't have to mind when the family start nibbling at them!

CHAPTER 10

Things Worth Growing

Flower arranging makes gardeners of us all even if, having no garden, we grow only a few indoor pot plants or have a couple of overflowing plant tubs on the balcony of a town flat. For the flower arranger who has a small garden the best advice certainly is "Grow shrubs and foliage plants." It is nearly always possible to buy flowers, but few shops stock the leaves which are so essential.

I do all my own gardening, so I can nurture the queerest-looking plants without question. All kinds of flowers and leaves are allowed to grow as they will, to give unexpected bends and twists which are an inspiration when I cut them for arranging.

Whether your picking garden is large or just a short border, be selective. Grow only those things which will be of value; ruthlessly throw out plants with poor quality blooms or inferior lasting properties. On the following pages are briefly listed some plants well worth growing. This is not a comprehensive list (for almost anything which grows can be useful to the flower arranger), and nurserymen's descriptive catalogues will supply you with countless other suggestions and give you information about cultivation.

ABUTILON MEGAPOTAMICUM (Flowering Maple). Rich red and gold dangling flowers through the summer months. A small shrub, rather tender, and must be taken indoors for the winter.

ACHILLEA (Milfoil or yarrow). Has round heads of golden flowers, which are excellent when dried for winter decoration. Gold Plate is a good, big variety.

ALCHEMILLA MOLLIS (Lady's Mantle). Has little green blossoms borne in airy sprays. The flowers are perfect for miniature arrangements, and the leaves ideal for masking pinholders and wire netting.

ALLIUM. There are many varieties of allium, providing pleasant flowers. My favourite is *A. cernuum*, which has blooms of exquisite tiny richly-coloured bells on arching stalks. There are well-shaped seedheads. Grow too, if you have the room, *A. albopilosum*, which has flowers that grow in lilac spheres, *A. azureum*, which is cornflower blue, and *A. giganteum*, which carries magnificent globular heads of pale violet-rose. *A. triquetrum* bears looser flowers in white with a green stripe.

ALSTRŒMERIA (Peruvian Lily). Has lily-like flowers with attractive markings, in many colours including pink, flame, coral, and orange. There are useful seedheads.

AMELANCHIER (Snowy Mespilus). Has three seasons of beauty, first when the opening leaves show pink, next when every branch is hung with white flowers, and finally in the autumn when the leaves turn a rich russet. A good variety is *A. canadensis*, which flowers in April or early May.

ANEMONE CORONARIA. A snowy-white flower on a tall stem, which blooms in spring.

ANGELICA. Large flower bosses, highly desirable for "all green" arrangements when the creamy flower has gone to seed. The seedheads can be dried.

ARISÆMA CANDIDISSIMUM. A bulb plant; flowers in

June or July. The blooms are like small arums, striped with pink and green inside.

ARUM ITALICUM (Italian Arum). Has large spear-shaped dark green leaves, handsomely marbled, which are most valuable in winter.

BEGONIA REX. I rear many varieties in pots in the windows of my home. All have magnificent foliage which adds richness to any flower design.

BERBERIS. There are a number of varieties of this shrub. Some are evergreen and blossom in spring, some colour well in the autumn, and others have attractive fruits and berries. Any is worth a place in the garden. Cut the mature growth for arranging.

BERGENIA (*Megasea* or Giant Saxifrage). Has leathery evergreen leaves which colour yellow, rose, or mahogany. Heads of rich pink blossoms in spring. The variety *B. cordifolia* was Gertrude Jekyll's favourite; its leaves take on purple colouring in winter. Another variety, *B. ligulata*, has near-white blossoms with rosy calyces.

BLEEDING HEART. Often called Lady's Locket, Seal Flower, Dutchman's Breeches, or Lady-in-the-Bath. Has a heart-shaped bud the colour of peppermint pink rock. This variety is *Dicentra spectabilis*. Smaller variety is *D. eximia*, while *D. alba* has white flowers.

BOCCONIA (Plume Poppy). I prize this plant more than orchids. It has grey-green indented leaves with grey-white undersides, and spires of peach-coloured buds and flowers.

BOUGAINVILLEA. My plant of this has grown happily, flowering every year, in my bedroom window. Each tiny flower has three lilac-coloured bracts, which make it highly desirable to the flower arranger, and which last very well. A climbing plant.

CATANANCHE CÆRULEA (Cupid's Dart). Has small mauve-blue long-lasting flowers. Its silver calyces dry on the plant and keep their colour for winter use if cut before autumn rains rot the stems. Unusual, if gilded, for the smaller Christmas arrangements.

CENTAUREA. A large-leafed perennial cornflower, quite distinct from the ordinary annual cornflower. I grow the variety *C. pulchra májor*, not only for its dull-green leaves with near-white undersides but also for the paper-like calyces which, when dried and included in autumn arrangements, never fail to set people talking. The blooms are purple-pink. *C. ruthenica* has citron-yellow flowers and fern-like leaves.

CLEMATIS. Did you know that it is possible to have one or another variety of clematis in flower, with luck, every month of the year? For January flowers plant *C. calycina*, which has single creamy-white bell flowers. *C. cirrhosa* has creamy-white hanging blooms which are produced in mild weather from February to April. Summer flowering varieties include Duchess of Edinburgh, a double white, tinted with green. *C. tangutica* has golden-yellow flowers and, like all clematis, a second period of charm when in seed. November and December may appear to be months without a clematis flower, but try *C. paniculata* in the shelter of a warm wall. Its small white blooms are vanilla-scented.

COBÆA SCANDENS (Cup and Saucer Vine). A normally quick-growing annual. Its purple and green flowers are shaped rather like those of the Canterbury Bell.

CONVOLVULUS CNEORUM (Shrubby Convolvulus). A

small bush of pleasant silver-grey foliage, with satin-white flowers finely striped with pink in late summer.

CORKSCREW HAZEL. The stems are treasured for the strange contorted shapes into which they twist and bend. Ideal for line arrangements.

CRINUM POWELLII (Cape Lily). A superb bulb plant, which has large trumpet-shaped blooms of pink. *C. powellii album* has white flowers.

CYCLAMEN NEAPOLITANUM. Everyone is enchanted with the miniature cyclamen flowers of this little beauty. Grown from corms, it is perfectly hardy and throws silvery marbled foliage.

DAPHNE. The variety *D. Mezereum*, a compact shrub, has purple-pink flowers and red berries. *D. Cneorum* is much smaller; has evergreen foliage and delicious shell-pink flower clusters.

DIERAMA (Wand Flower or Venus's Fishing Rod). Has arching wiry stems which tremble in every breeze and carry little rose-pink flowers in clusters. Good seed-heads.

DIGITALIS. The common foxglove—and I wouldn't be without it in my garden. Apart from the blooms, I use its green seed capsules in late summer to create interesting outline shapes, and in the autumn the spent seedheads can be dried. The seedheads can also be gilded for Christmas designs. The variety called *Ambigua* has lovely yellow flowers.

DORONICUM (Leopard's Bane). This golden flower is among the first herbaceous plants to bloom in spring and stays in flower for several months.

ELÆAGNUS. I grow the variety *Pungens Variegata*, which

has glossy evergreen leaves splashed with gold. *E. macrophylla* and *E. ebingii* are also grown for their richly-coloured foliage.

EPIMEDIUM (Barrenwort). Has sweet little flowers like tiny columbines, in various colours and many varieties. *E. perralderianum* has yellow flowers and leaves which tint in autumn and winter; *E. rubrum* has crimson blooms and foliage tinted in spring; *E. versicolor sulphureum* presents its spring leaves blotched with brown.

EREMURUS (Foxtail Lily). A good variety is *E. robustus*, which grows to six or eight feet tall. Its flowers are pink; other varieties have blooms of white, apricot, maize yellow, and soft orange. The flowers grow on in water after cutting.

ERICA. It is impossible to list all the hardy heathers, all useful for flower arranging, but a worthwhile variety is the popular H. E. Beale, which has lengthy spikes of double flowers of a soft rose colour. The various winter-flowering heathers are a "must," and at least one tree heather should be grown.

ERYNGIUM MARITIMUM (Sea Holly). Has grey calyces which can be dried. The variety *Giganteum*, popularly known as Miss Willmott's Ghost, is a biennial with blue flowers and a grey-white prickly ruff.

ERYTHRONIUM DENS-CANIS. Like me, you'll probably know this better as Dog's Tooth Violet. It flowers in the springtime and makes an attractive addition to the rock garden. Snowflake is the name of a white-flowered form. *E. revolutum* (White Beauty) has mottled foliage and big white flowers with yellow centres. *E. tuolumnense* produces taller stems with deep yellow blooms.

EUCALYPTUS. Grown for its beautiful grey foliage and

young leaves flushed with pink. The variety *E. gunnii* is the hardiest, but *E. globulus* is also worth growing.

EUPHORBIA (Spurge). Has rather strange yellow-green blooms. *E. wulfenii* has handsome foliage and large stems thickly massed with flowers. *E. characias* is bigger, and also shows its croziers all winter. In the spring its green flower has a maroon eye.

EVERLASTING PEA (*Lathyrus latifolius*). A perennial which blooms in rose-pink or white and climbs like a sweet pea.

FRITILLARIA (Snake's Head Lily). Grown from a bulb, its distinctive white and purple flowers have strange chequered markings. *F. citrina* is a more unusual form stocked by some nurseries; it has dainty yellow flowers. *F. meleagris alba* is pure white.

GALTONIA (*Hyacinthus candicans*).) A stately plant which provides white flowers. The hyacinth-like blooms grow all round a graceful green stem. Individual florets can be cut. *G. princeps* has flowers of soft jade green. Interesting seedheads.

GARRYA ELLIPTICA. An evergreen with dangling green catkins useful for winter arrangements. Its common name of Silk Tassel Bush is a good description.

GLADIOLUS. Do grow the smaller gladioli, such as the Butterfly and the Primulinus. The bigger varieties are usually too large for everyday use, but the smaller ones are more than useful. Butterfly varieties which I like include Femina (a delightful peach-pink with scarlet markings to the throat); Ice Follies, one of the best whites (it has an amber blotch); Jolly Jokers (creamy yellow); and Desirée (deep scarlet). The ruffled miniature gladioli are not so tall as the Butterflies and they bear smaller flowers.

Bo-Peep is one of the oldest and is buff-pink with a touch of red at the throat. Peter Pan is orange, apricot, and yellow; Parfait is salmon and cream; and Tony Boy is rose and creamy-white. Emily's Birthday is an early flowering variety with petals of apricot-pink. The Primulinus hybrids include Massasoit (bright scarlet); Pegasus (creamy-white with a red line); Rainbow Falls (lilac-pink with a white throat); and Ocean Spray (creamy white with an amber blotch).

HELLEBORUS. The Lenten Rose comes in several varieties. *H. Corsicus* has handsome evergreen leaves and spring clusters of pale green blossoms. *H. viridis* also has green flowers. The name *Helleborus orientalis* covers many hybrids varying from plum colour to blush, usually spotted with maroon within the petals. The petals thicken and turn green as summer comes, and the slow-forming seedheads make fascinating additions to choice designs. The variety *H. niger* is the well-known Christmas Rose.

HEUCHERA. Sometimes called Coral Bells, but can also be obtained with white, green, pink, and red flowers. *H. rubescens* has dainty sprays of greenish flowers and young leaves of a copper colour.

HIMALAYAN POPPY (*Meconopsis*). A plant of outstanding beauty. Its azure flowers cause a stir when used in an arrangement.

HONESTY. The disc-shaped silver centres of the seedpods are well-known, and these are also useful in their green state. A perennial variety, *Lunaria redivava*, has lilac flowers.

HOSTA (Funkia or Plantain Lily). Has many lovely varieties, one of which has leaves of clear yellow-green. Another is gaily striped with white like an awning, and a third has foliage of butter-yellow and green.

HOUSELEEK. There are well over a hundred varieties of the *Sempervivum*. My collection of about 20 ranges in colour from sulphur yellow through bronze, purple, and green to a rich ruby-red.

HOYA CARNOSA (Honey-plant). I grow this in my sunny bedroom window from spring to autumn, and in the heated bathroom in the winter. Has wax-like blooms in early summer, each individual bloom carrying a single drop of nectar which reflects the light.

IVY. Grow any of the many varieties of ivy indoors or outdoors—they are always welcome, especially the variegated kinds. Trails of small leaves picked in autumn or winter will dry perfectly, retaining their infinite variations of colour.

KALMIA LATIFOLIA (Calico Bush or Icing Sugar Bush). Has indescribably lovely "iced" rosettes of pink, white and rose-red.

LACHENALIA. A graceful indoor plant flowering in spring with spires of tubular-shaped blooms. Colours range from green to coral and gold, and most are jade green in bud. The flowers last for many weeks in water if picked when in bud.

LAVATERA. Useful blossoms, like mallow, of a rich pink. The annual *lavatera* will grow in almost any soil in an open sunny place.

LAVENDER. Two pleasing varieties are Hidcote Pink (a clear pink colour) and Vera, which has blooms in a very pale lavender tint.

LEUCOJUM VERNUM. The Spring Snowflake, produces white flowers which are tipped with green. *L. aestivum* is called the Summer Snowflake.

Lewisia. A rock plant with fine flower sprays. Colours include pink, peach, and apricot.

Lily. All the many varieties of the lily are beautiful. *L. giganteum* can grow as tall as a man and has drooping white flowers perhaps up to ten inches long. Its dried seedheads are attractive. *L. Martagon* has a delicate little flower with turned-back petals in purple or white. *L. auratum* has golden-rayed blooms, and *L. speciosum* has crimson-spotted flowers. Try also *L. longiflorum* (Easter Lily) and *L. candidum* (Madonna Lily).

Linaria (Yellow Toad Flax). A wild perennial which I like so much that I grow it in the garden. There are also a number of annual and perennial varieties cultivated for cut flowers. The blooms are like tiny snapdragons.

Lungwort (*Pulmonaria*). Called Soldiers and Sailors because of its pink and blue flowers on the one plant. The variety *P. saccharata* has marbled foliage. I also grow *P. rubra*, which has coral-red bells, and in a mild winter I sometimes pick the first flowers in January.

Mexican Orange (*Choisya ternata*). An evergreen with glossy foliage and fragrant white flowers.

Muscari (Grape Hyacinth). Takes its name from the Greek word for a cluster or bunch of grapes. There is a white-flowered form, *Alba*, which is not so common to-day but which was very widely grown in Elizabethan times, when it was called Pearls of Spain. The variety *M. plumosum* bears long-lasting heads of soft violet-purple, and its unusual flowers are like feathered plumes. Flowering is in May.

Myrtle. A useful evergreen shrub with small white flowers. Can be grown indoors.

Narcissus. There are a number of varieties. I like

Cyclamineus Beryl, primrose-coloured with a small orange cup. Peeping Tom has a long, deep yellow trumpet; Trevithian has a broad pale lemon-yellow perianth and a shallow crown; Silver Chimes carries sweetly-scented heads of six or more flowers, lemon and white. The variety W. P. Milner gives small sulphur-yellow daffodils.

NIGELLA (Love-in-a-Mist). As well as growing the common blue variety, do spare a little space for a new pink one, Monarch Persian Rose.

ORNAMENTAL CABBAGE AND KALE. Firm favourites with flower arrangers. The cabbages are soft green and cream, rose-pink, fuchsia-pink, and cerise. The kale, in similar colours, can be cultivated as a perennial if cut back and not allowed to flower. I have some plants in my garden which are four years old.

OSMUNDA FERN (Royal Fern). Beautiful in spring, when arrangements of great distinction can be produced with its copper-tinted croziers. Can be pressed and kept for winter use.

PASSIFLORA (Passion Flower). A distinctive climber whose curious flowers need no description. Worth having is the pure white variety named Constance Elliott.

PHALARIS ARUNDINACEA VARIEGATA. A long name for the well-known variegated ribbon grass with the country name of Gardener's Garters.

PHLOMIS SAMIA (Jerusalem Sage). Has yellow flowers which perhaps look most attractive when the leaves are carefully removed from the stems so that the flowers are clearly seen.

PHORMIUM VARIEGATUM (New Zealand Flax). Has striking leaves like green swords with yellow stripes running the full length. A wonderful ingredient in really big arrangements.

PIERIS FORMOSA FORRESTII. A shrub with new growths of brilliant crimson, rather like poinsettia.

PLUMBAGO CAPENSIS (Cape Leadwort). A wall shrub from South Africa bearing clusters of delicate blue flowers which resemble tiny phlox. I grow it in an upstairs window.

POPPY. Poppies of any variety are never wasted in the flower arranger's garden, and if left unstaked will assume interesting natural curves. Cut the stems long, and dry the seedheads for winter use.

POTENTILLA (Cinquefoil). I grow this instead of geum; its flower is similar to geum but the petals don't drop so easily. Gibson's Scarlet is attractive.

PRUNUS SUBHIRTELLA AUTUMNALIS (Autumn Cherry). Should be in every garden. My pink one flowers twice in the autumn, during fine spells in the winter, and again in the spring. There is also a white variety.

ROSES. You can never have too many roses, especially the varieties with subdued and subtle colourings. Impossible to list them all, but do try Café, a pale brown rose which accompanies orange-yellow blooms to perfection. For something really out of the ordinary grow *Rosa chinensis viridiflora;* its odd (green-brown) petals, which are really sepals are so distinctive and of great usefulness, especially in the autumn when teamed with orange berries, dahlias and chrysanthemums. There are roses with wonderful colourings of amethyst, grey-mauve and rose lilac—varieties such as Twilight, Overture, Lilac Charm, and Lilac Time. The variety Magenta produces heavy trusses of magenta-hued blooms, the shades of which change every day as the rose matures. I grow this with one it complements so well, Lavender Pinocchio. Among a small collection of old shrub roses I have Louise Odier and Madame Pierre Oger, both of which have curving shell-like petals of great beauty; Cardinal Richelieu (deep mauve-grey flowerheads); and another favourite of mine, Pink Grootendorst, which often obliges with a second flowering in the autumn. Some roses are worth cultivating for their leaves, fruits, or thorns. For example, *Rosa rubriflora* has long sprays of remarkable little leaves of a soft slate-blue shade and little dark cherry-red hips. *Rosa Moyesii* has dusky red flowers followed by shapely hips, while *Rosa omiensis* is noteworthy for its translucent red thorns. Miniature roses grow in the garden and will provide dozens of perfect little blooms throughout the summer.

RUE (Herb of Grace). Grow the variety Jackman's Blue, a superior grey-blue shade. Leaves, flowers, and seedheads of rue are all valuable. The Meadow Rue (Thalictrum, Hewitt's Double) has graceful stems and showers of tiny lavender-tinted pom-poms.

SARCOCOCCA. A small shrub with narrow, erect leaves, and tiny pink flowers in January.

SHASTA DAISY. These days the double and semi-double forms of the ordinary garden ox-eye or dog daisy are a "must" for flower arrangers. They last extremely well when cut, and have a long flowering period. The variety named Esther Read is the most commonly grown, but there are others. John Murray is an excellent one, as is Ben Lomond.

SOLOMON'S SEAL (*Polygonatum*). Sometimes called Jingling Johnny. Has gracefully arching stems carrying small creamy white tubular flowers which hang downwards like little bells. The lovely green leaves which accompany the flowers are sometimes removed by flower arrangers who find that the delicate bell-hung stems take on a more fragile appearance without them. A big and very striking variety is *Polygonatum multiflorum*.

STREPTOCARPUS (Cape Primrose). A house plant which can be "struck" from a leaf. Fleshy-leafed and velvet-petalled, it flowers for months. It has trumpet-shaped blue, pink, or white blooms in loose sprays. The white and pink varieties bear a marked resemblance to orchids. My favourite is lavender, veined with royal purple and colouring suddenly at the throat to primrose yellow.

TELLIMA GRANDIFLORA. A green flower for spring use. Delightful fringed bells on foot-high stems, and appealing leaves of green with bronze markings in winter.

TIARELLA. The variety *T. cordifolia* has spikes of white flowers like little bottle brushes. *T. wherryi* has flowers of a soft apricot colour, and is scented. Both varieties bloom in spring.

TULIPS. The name is said to be derived from the flower's resemblance to the Eastern headdress called "tulipan" or "turban," though the resemblance is not so strong in some of the newer varieties. Perfect for flower arranging are the long petalled lily-flowered varieties, which have an elegant manner of growth. New strains bred from the green, flowered *Tulipa viridiflora* have been quickly acclaimed by flower arrangers. I find that the variety called Artist flourishes well in my garden, where six bulbs have made nearly three times as many in a few years. This sturdy tulip is coloured terra-cotta and green. *T. Formosa* is almost green, while Greenland has a flush of deep rose. Notable for their brilliant interlacing of colours are the Bybloem, Bizarre, and Rembrandt tulips. The variety called Bright Interval has a large flower of cherry-pink overlaid with creamy white splashes, while Insulinde has a charming contrast of colours—yellow, bronze, deep purple and various shades of mahogany on a primrose ground. Another Bizarre variety, named Zebra, combines soft crimson with primrose-yellow, and its open blooms are rich mahogany with streaks of clear yellow.

WILD FLOWERS. Many wild flowers are becoming more difficult to find in their natural state; keep a corner of the garden for growing roots of any you can find. A treasure is Wild Arum (Cuckoo Pint, or Lords and Ladies) with its dark green arrow-shaped leaves which are often spotted with purple or streaked with a lighter colour. The flowers are handsome and are followed by orange-red berries. Even the flower arranger without a garden can pick a great many interesting leaves, grasses, seedheads and berries from the hedgerows, waste ground, common, or heathland, or just the roadside verges. Wild fungi can be very colourful and shapely, and can be dried in borax and used over and over again. Some wild plants worth looking out for are yellow toad flax, dock, wild roses, foxgloves, wild hop, wild privet, honeysuckle, dead-nettle, scabious, purple loose-strife, heather, and the leaves, flowers, and fruits of many trees.

No one can give you a full list of the natural material it is possible to use in flower arranging; the important thing is to develop your own "seeing eye" so that you always visualise the potentialities of the material you have at hand.

Index

*The asterisked page numbers * refer to illustrations*